Around Horton
and Longsdon

Heath family at Fields Farm, Gratton c.1902.

Compiled by Sheila Hine

Front cover: Harry Wooliscroft. Back cover: Horton Church and The Clews Family

ACKNOWLEDGEMENTS
Thank you to my parents for their help, especially Dad.
Thank you to everyone who has contributed in any way, those named and their families,
and Eileen Harvey, the Embrey family and Bob & Theresa Stubbs.

CHURNET VALLEY BOOKS
1 King Street, Leek, Staffordshire. ST13 5NW 01538 399033 www.leekbooks.co.uk
© Sheila Hine and Churnet Valley Books 2009 ISBN 9781904546627

Brian Shufflebotham

I was born in 1933 at Bradshaw Park, Devils Lane, Longsdon; the third child of Garnet and Margaret (nee Turnock) Shufflebotham, both surnames well rooted in North Staffordshire and North Cheshire and especially in the parishes of Horton and Longsdon.

The origin of these names could be that Shufflebothams are descendants of sheep herders housed out on the open range in a small hut on wheels or skids and spoken of as a sheep man in his 'bytham' or 'bothie'. In the time of Henry VIII, the name was spelt 'Sheplebotham'. It is said that 'Turnock' was derived from craftsmen who were 'turners of oak'. There may be other claims, but I am quite happy to settle upon these here.

Along the way, through marriage, it is claimed both our Shufflebotham and Turnock bloodlines joined with descendants of the aristocracy! Threads to this are on my mother's Turnock family side through William the Conqueror's nobleman Bertram de Verdun. I am told Croxden Abbey was built by his grandson, also Bertram (1153-1192) who dedicated it 'for the good of the souls of Norman my father and Lascelline my mother' and that in 1508, a certain Thomas Endon said to be a descendant of the founder of Croxden Abbey, entered the Abbey here and stayed there until the Dissolution.

In 1673, another Thomas Endon purchased Dairy House, Horton, built in 1635 by Richard Biddulph. A Catholic Royalist family, its subsequent owner, John Biddulph was killed at the battle of Hopton Heath and the house sequestered by the Parliamentarians. In 1681, Elizabeth, sister of Thomas Endon, very wisely for us married Thomas Turnock, my five times great grandfather.

Dairy House, described as a two cross wings house, has on the front a sculptured stone with the initials for Jesus and Virgin Mary, and on the service part, initials for John (Biddulph) and his wife Mary (nee Eyre).

After their marriage in 1681, Thomas and Elizabeth Turnock resided there with Elizabeth's brother Thomas Endon. A great grandson, Thomas Endon Turnock (1768-1795) resided at Dairy

House. Other names found living there include a William Yardley who used it as a Quaker meeting house and was imprisoned for a time for speaking out in Leek Parish Church. There is a William Pilsbury, a James Lockett, the Bostock family, Richard Myatt, George Robinson and his family, until in the Victorian period we have another Turnock of our family as the landlord. This Richard Turnock, silk manufacturer, on his death in 1909 left it in his will to his brother, my grandad, William Turnock who had moved to the farm in 1891.

It is claimed that all with the surname of Brindley worldwide descend from a single family who originally occupied the one location in Cheshire named Brindley and who descended from Norman noble landowner Brundelegh de Brindley.

Much further down, descendants include the famous canal engineer James Brindley who had daughters only, so no-one named Brindley is directly descended from him. However, the youngest of his three brothers was

Joseph Brindley of Rough Hey Farm.
Nephew of James Brindley.

Dairy House Farm.

Rear of Dairy House
Farm.

I.J.B. Shufflebotham
and Mrs Shufflebotham
with Garnet at
Bradshaw Mount.

My grandparents Mary Jane
Poole of Heath House,
Horton and I.J.B.
Shufflebotham.

Henry Brindley (1734-1810) who had 6 sons and 3 daughters. A son named Joseph (1769-1848) lived at Rough Hey Farm, Gawsworth and his daughter Mary Brindley married a William Webster Winkle. Their daughter Judith married Richard Shufflebotham - my great grandparents.

Richard Shufflebotham in 1860 was appointed the surveyor of the Turnpike from Congleton to Hartington. His letters of appointment are at the Stafford County Records Office. Richard and Judith also lived at Wincle Grange Farm and at Whitelea Farm, Wincle and Brook House Farm, Mottram St.Andrew, before finally ending their days at Little Bradshaw Farm, Longsdon; where they lived with their son, Isaac Joseph Brindley Shufflebotham, affectionately known as 'IJB'. In 1902, IJB commissioned and had built the private house on Dunwood Road known as 'Bradshaw Mount'. Pausing as you go by this house, you will see his initials above the front door. He was chairman of the Leek RDC in 1909.

My father, Garnet was born at Little Bradshaw Farm in 1898 and educated at Longsdon Primary School and the Leek Nicholson Institute School. His father owned a property in the Macclesfield Parliamentary Division and so had a vote in both that area and at Leek. Father told me of the occasion when as a young lad he went with his dad by pony and trap to Wincle School for his father to vote and on the return journey they stopped at the Ship Inn where he had ham and for the first time in his life with two eggs!

In the First World War, at 18, he trained with the 10th Hussars before being posted to France joining No.2 Troop A Squadron, 20th Hussars. He spoke very little of his service life conceding only once of having lost more than one horse. After his death, a historical record of the service of his squadron revealed involvement in some horrendous

Garnet at Aldershot Barracks 1917.

skirmishes both as cavalry and in the trenches. Finally we found that in August 1918 in the battle of Amiens, on an 11 mile front with 2,070 allied guns, suffering 22,000 British and 20,000 French casualties, his squadron were in the action. My father was gassed and invalided out after being admitted to a hospital at Tidworth on the 8th September of that year.

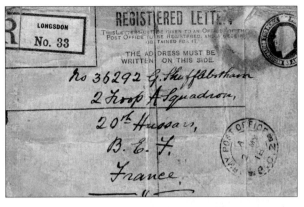

With one lung completely destroyed, when he married my mother, she related being told by his doctor not to expect him to live a long life! She died in 1976, dad lived on to 1983 aged 85.

My mother Margaret (1901-1976) lived at Dairy House and for some of her teenage years she remained working at home and along with her older sister Jessie helped their mum until she died in 1916, when the youngest of their 9 brothers was aged 4. She told me of the times they baked cakes for their brothers and charged them 1d a cake.

I have an umbrella of my mother's, which she first acquired when courting. My father told how she would be carrying this when they met along some footpath between Dairy House and Bradshaw Mount. It's certainly a treasured keepsake of mine.

Alongside his business of being a poultry and livestock farmer at Bradshaw Park, from 1937 my father gave a great deal of unpaid public service over a period of 40 years or so. This included 34 years on the Leek Rural District Council and similarly on Longsdon Parish Council. Along with a stint as Chairman of both, he was honorary clerk of Longsdon PC for 21 years. He was County Councillor for the Rudyard Division and in 1974 an Alderman of the County Council until local government reorganisation did away with this office. For a time he was chairman of the Poultry Association of Great Britain.

In the Second World War, my older sister Jean enrolled with the WAAF. Her service duties were mainly in transport and as a driver at times on the airfield ambulance, bringing in injured flying personnel and some who had not survived. For her military service, Jean received a 'Mention in Dispatches' and for this wears an Oak Leaf on her War Medal.

My elder brother, Derek was tragically killed, aged 17 in 1948 on the Whit bank holiday in an accident with his 250cc BSA motorbike on a corner by Taylors Green Farm at Dunwood. The corner was subsequently widened. In those days, literally hundreds if not thousands of pedal cyclists streamed out of the Potteries to Rudyard. They could occupy the full width of the road in packs and droves, bells ringing and with much shouting as they joyously made the journey. Unfortunately for Derek, he met a pack on what was then a blind corner with a young lad peddling like billy-ho and cutting the corner to catch up with his uncle. Witnesses said that had Derek been travelling at anything but a slow speed, then he would have killed the child. Instead he slewed his motorbike to the right and its weight simply laid him down on the road grazing his temple. Dazed, he was admitted by ambulance to the Leek Cottage Hospital. That evening, father took his pyjamas in only to return with them in his hands around 10pm and the devastating news that Derek had died as a consequence of brain damage. Had he been wearing a crash helmet, which in those days was not compulsory, he would have survived. My younger brother, Michael took up the reins of the family farm business until he retired.

There were no school buses to my knowledge and I have no recollection of being accompanied or transported to school by my parents or anyone. The 'school run' had yet to be invented, though I remember occasions when attending Longsdon Primary School with my friend Reg Hill that his mum sometimes met us halfway along Devils Lane. Reg lived at Gibraltar Farm and I remember calling for him and sometimes, he had still to have his breakfast. Whereas at Bradshaw Park we had electricity, they didn't at Gibraltar. His mum would be cooking breakfast using a frying pan on their open leaded fire. I can drool to this day thinking about those eggs and bacon sizzling away in her frying pan!

Aged 9, I transferred to Leek High School, walking or cycling to the main road at Longsdon and catching the service bus, or sometimes cycling all the way. There always seemed to be people queuing at the bus stop; some buses went by without stopping, absolutely full. Mixed in between were numbers of Chatterley Whitfield coal lorries, perhaps little more than 5 or 7 ton gross, grinding their way through Longsdon en route to the Leek Gas Works.

I remember in the war period seeing the Leek Railway Station yard full of American troops arriving from Liverpool and setting off up through Leek to the Blackshaw Moor camp. I saw them at times being force marched through Longsdon pouring with sweat and the vehicle convoys wending their way along Devils Lane on practice journeys of some sort. Occasionally they would throw an empty cigarette packet to us or even gum; it was a collector's item for us at the time.

We could hear the air raid siren in Leek going off at Bradshaw Park, and the drone of aircraft - up and down drone was a German and a straight burr was British. My father would be out on Civil Defence duties and I remember mother standing outside watching the glow over Manchester and Liverpool as those cities were bombed.

On one occasion, in about 1942 or 43, just before blackout time, when we had still to draw down our roller blinds, there was the almighty roar of an aircraft skimming over our house. There had been no siren, mother shouted *'Draw the blinds!'* it frightened us nearly to death. A while later in pitch black dark, a loud knock came at our door. Mother took a peep, moving the blind and I remember feeling terrified! It was some airman or soldier. Father went to a drawer and took out a revolver. Holding it down by his side he went to the door, opened it and was confronted by this tall airman in flying gear, helmet and all. There was huge relief that he was British and it transpired that he was on a Spitfire training mission, was lost and had put down, landing in a field at Little Bradshaw Farm. Father telephoned and a short while later, the village policeman arrived and escorted the pilot away - this after mother had fed him well. I have never ceased to marvel at the experience of the pilot, of firstly having to land and to have then in total darkness with no lights anywhere and on foot scrambling his way up the steep woodland off the Dunwood Road and finding our house.

One Christmas Eve in the dead of night, we were awakened by the sound of a rough tractor-like engine which abruptly stopped and a moment later a thud. It unsettled us and I never forgot dad calling out, *'It's only Santa dropping his bag'*. It was nothing of the sort, but proved to be German 'doodle bugs' being dropped on Manchester that evening - some Santa!

I remember in the 1940s the Mill Pond on Devils Lane being frozen over and people coming from Longsdon to skate on it. My sister, serving in the WAAF, on leave invariably came home with a serviceman boyfriend. One brought us the gift of a single person RAF inflatable dinghy. We used to blow this up and float around on it on the Mill Pond. Heaven knows what would have happened had it deflated as I was a non-swimmer; or if we had gone through the ice in winter.

Longsdon School 1905/6. 1. Frank Owen, 2. Garnet Shufflebotham, 3. May Franklin, 4. Tom Myatt,
5. Violet Owen, 6. Alice Stubbs, 7. Miss Burrows.

Horton School. Margaret Turnock as Queen.

On the brow of the hill above Bradshaw Mount, before food rationing, Mrs Gritton, wife of the village postman Harry, on summer bank holidays had a tricycle ice cream cart. Harry delivered the post around the area on his pedal cycle which he lifted over stiles on the footpaths. He finished up needing an operation to correct the wear on his bag-carrying shoulder. They lived at Bradshaw Cottage and he was village postman for over 30 years.

On the track down from Summerhill nearby there was a small wooden hut occupied by Arthur Barber the cobbler. We used to spend many happy hours there keeping him company around his coke stove, chatting away as he repaired ours and other people's shoes. The front light on his bike was carbide operated.

As a young lad, I spent hours and hours across at Lapwing Farm, our neighbours, in the oil lamplight playing snakes and ladders and ludo with old man Lomas, a retired stonemason from Buxton who was deaf. They had no electricity, telephone or mains water. Their drinking water was fetched from a well in our wood, mostly by Mrs Lomas using a yoke with two buckets. Every now and then you would see them off to Longsdon to the shop, travelling by pony and trap.

Lapwing Farmhouse, since demolished and replaced.

I remember the coal-fired steamroller patching Devils lane. There was a local road lengthsman by the name of Harry Crombie who looked after the ditches and road gulleys around our area and kept the lanes tidy.

There was a time when my mother must have been very ill and confined to bed for weeks on end. Every so many days we were dispatched laden with baskets to walk over the woodland down to the Dunwood road and up to Horton to the Crown Inn, where our Uncle Fred and Aunty Ethel Turnock were the licensees, before the pub had a bar. I seem to recall a sort of hallway with seats down the side and Uncle Fred fetched drinks out to customers sitting there. Aunty Ethel did the washing of our clothes and sent us back with her home baking. Laden down we trundled homewards. I was about 10 at the time.

I remember aged about 11 at Christmas collecting branches of holly out of our woodland and on a sledge hauling it into Leek to stand by Woolworths and very quickly sold out, returning home with a pocketful of pennies.

I remember going with father transporting railway Hessian sacks of wheat to Harracles Mill at Rudyard for grinding. We saw Mr Bailey, the operator, in periods of dry weather coming up to the Mill Pond to lift a plank or two at the overflow to release water downstream to operate the mill. We would fish for sticklebacks in the brook.

On our farm, we did not have a bull and with no AI then, with a cow coming into service, the practice was to walk it to the neighbour Joe Embrey at Rowley Gate to his bull. I was once picking mushrooms in the area and when having dropped over a quite high dry stone wall, I found myself in the field with a less than friendly looking bull. I doubt if I have ever run so fast in my life or gone over a wall so quickly!

Joe Embrey with his flying 'Tippler', Best Bird at Crystal Palace Show 1928 and 1929, and winner of 30 first prizes.

Joe with shorthorn bull.

Joe Embrey was a leading light in the Leek Fur and Feather Club and a pigeon fancier. He had one pigeon loft up some granary steps and it was a real treat for us lads when he proudly showed us his pigeons.

I remember in 1944 hearing a plane exercising over in the direction of Bagnall, then all was quiet after a loud bang. It was a summer afternoon and mother commented, 'He's crashed'. A short while later, we saw a parachute drifting over, on the Dunwood side of the farm. She hurried in to fetch the binoculars and called to father that the parachutist was doing nothing, just drifting. He landed in a field just above Steele House. Derek and myself ran down through our wood to Lyme House and along the Dunwood

St James School, Longsdon. The building was the Mission church before St Chad's was built. (see p. 127)

Road to where he was. People had gathered round where he lay there calling for a doctor. They assured him that a doctor was coming but it was in vain as this US airman died. In later years, I have reflected when the USA is criticised for involvement in conflicts in other countries, of that young airman in 1944, having parents at home possibly thinking, *'Why should our son be over there getting killed?'*

A war years' slogan was 'Dig for Victory' and we had an extra two weeks holiday in the autumn, which I spent working for my uncle, Arnold Turnock at Dairy House. I cycled there via the unmade Moss Road, now Tollgate Road and up to Horton. We went to some far fields first to harvest the potato crop. The horse drawn spinner went first, then we picked the spuds into baskets and loaded them into horse-drawn carts. Next it was the mangolds; topping and tailing and what a back-aching job that was. For lunch we went back to the house where we tucked in to a right good farmer's dinner and then back to the field. Uncle Arnold paid me one shilling a day for 10 days, I thus earned 10 bob - a small fortune, compared with the 6d a week pocket money I was receiving then.

Horton Harvest Festival was always a family occasion and we would all go to the morning service and usually followed by having our Sunday dinner at Coney Greave Farm, the home of our Uncle Samuel and Aunty Charlotte Turnock.

After the Normandy landings, the Blackshaw Moor camps were vacated by the American troops and next came the Italian POWs. Small groups used to be out walking along Devils Lane. On one occasion, by the entrance to Rowley Gate Farm, we were out playing and met some of them resting on the verge. They gathered up some willow shoots and there and then weaved us a basket that we proudly took home to mum.

In the 1947 winter, we hardly missed a day at school. Devils Lane was closed for weeks, but by zigzagging via gates across the fields, we made it to Longsdon cross-roads. If the buses were not running we walked the rest of the way. Sometimes in inclement weather, mother would give us the choice of either going to school or if staying at home to clean out the free-range hencotes with wheelbarrow and shovel. We opted mostly for school!

At 17, I attended a winter residential course at the Rodbaston Farm Institute and at 18 received my call up papers for National Service. Being a farmer's lad and mindful of my father's war service and emphasising my ability to drive a tractor, I asked if I might be sent to join an armoured Hussar tank regiment. Papers instead came for the Royal Army Ordnance Corps. After initial training at Aldershot, leading to becoming a 'marksman' with the .303 rifle and qualifying as a drill and LMG (light machine gun) weapon training instructor and specifying that as a farmer's lad I wished to have a permanent outside role, the War Office eventually posted me to the massive Base Ordnance Depot at Bicester and here trained me as a clerk, where I finished up as a Sergeant supervising some 45,000 stores account records and transactions. On demob, dad said, *'I think you had better be a secretary.'* And the rest is history, my finishing up doing 43 years as an NFU secretary.

Remembrance Sunday 1952.
Brian, with his sister and father.

Willow House, Leek Road, Longsdon in Edwardian times, demolished and replaced 1967. *Photo courtesy of Mrs Lorna Bills.*

Below: At Willow House.

Minnie Gertrude Shufflebotham, music teacher, Willow House, Longsdon.

Florrie Fernyhough

I was born at Waterfall; we were on a rented farm. There were 7 of us children and mother died young when we were all little; I was only 5 and my youngest sister was 7 months old. Dad's sister, Aunty Ginny came to look after us but then she died and we were left with nobody; we had housekeepers but they didn't last long, so the family was split up, dad and three of them went to live at Roche Grange at Meerbrook and I ended up with another aunt at Rushton. It was very hard, I was sent to bed at night and used to cry and cry. They told me that when they had foot and mouth at Roche Grange and all the animals were killed, my sisters were upset when they killed the pet lamb. There was no compensation then.

I left Rushton School at 14 and worked in a mill for a while, winding silk. Then I went into farm service. My sister got me jobs; she worked at Bond House, Horton for Abel Heath. I was at Park House for Arthur Heath then went to Green Tree.

I got married to Jack and we farmed at Fernyhill, Bradnop on a rented farm, then we had a sale there and bought this farm, Fenton Fields for £6,000, it was 29 acres and everyone said Jack was mad! I've lived here for over 60 years.

We kept 20 cows and a pig or two; you could make a living out of it then. Then the Water Board took 9 acres off us for the reservoir; it was compulsory purchased at £150 an acre. It was to store 10 million gallons of water for the Potteries; there was already an old reservoir behind but it never held water. It was 1963 when they built it, they let us rent some land back which they took from other farms or we couldn't have gone on.

John Fernyhough

I used to do a bit of agricultural contracting and one day I was baling for Percy Nixon at the bottom of Honeysuckle Lane. I'd done 5$^{1}/_{2}$ acres and got half an acre left when my baler packed up. I said to Perce, *'There in't a lot left.'* He'd got a small Bamford baler of his own. *'I'll go fetch that, Perce.'* *'Neah, dunner fetch that,'* he says. *'It's too slow; go and borrer Roy's.'* *'Neahr, Roy's'll be busy,'* I said, and I went and fetched the Bamford to the field. When I got back he came pounding down the field to me - I could see summat were up. He went to th' string box, lifted lid up and said. *'Oh, thank God fer that.'*

He'd got his money box in there. He kept it in there because he didn't like keeping it in the house 'cus he'd got no key for the house door. I said, *'How come?'* He said that Johnny had chucked it away in the holly bushes. Well, Johnny were getting on for thirty odd. I said, *'That's a funny thing do.'* He said, *'Oh, I dunner mean now, it'd be when he were 4 year old; he threw it away in a temper one day and I've never been able find it and we've never locked door ever since.'*

Another day I was helping our relations at Stanlow combining corn. I was bagging away. Hughie Dawson came and he was taking the bags off with the tractor and loader and I was riding on tying the bags up. Just now Gladys comes across with sustenance for us. She'd got a jug of coffee and mugs in a basket and started tipping it out into the mugs and it went plop, plop. The milk was sour before she'd started of it. I already knew that one of the drivers on the Co-op wagon had called at our farm and said, *'I've got some milk back for you - rejected, red labels on top o' th' lid.'* I looked and said, *'It's not mine.'* It was for Stanlow. *'Neahr,'* he said, *'I'm pullin' your leg.'* It was this here milk, she'd made coffee of it and it had landed across to us.

Fenton Fields about 1920.

John and Jack Fernyhough at Fenton Fields.

Alison, Derek & Phillip Heath at Broadmeadows, Horton.

Dick Heath

When I was a kid, we lived at The Hollins at Horton, then we moved to Dams Lane so I went to school at Horton - Owd Leech was teacher. He lived across Rudyard Green Lane. A couple of us lads, we used to have fetch his washin' and take it to Mrs Shufflebottom up Lask Edge and then tak' it back. It didner matter how long it took, it got you out of school. It was wrapped up in a ball and we used to roll it down the hills; it was mucky lookin' when we'd finished.

Sam Bennison was my mate - we used sneak off and catch trout in the Horton Brook. You get thee hand underneath and throw 'em out no trouble, I was quite good at it.

The farmers used leave milk churns at the lane end near the school and the lads would tie the empty ones up in the trees so they struggled find 'em. I went to live at Park House, I was farmed out to Uncle Arthur, helping him on the farm and still going to school while his lads were too young to help. Then when we went to Bradshaw I left school and went to work for Jack Myatt at Lyme House.

Arthur Barber lived in the wood near Summerhill in a shed. It was raining very hard one night so me and Jack Dickinson rolled some big stones to the door so he couldn't get in then we hid and waited to hear him cossin'. Sometimes we stuffed his chimney up. He was a good cobbler and

he used mend our binder canvas, but he'd be that drunk, he'd fall on them and break the wooden laths. He had put no end o' tin tacks in to hold 'em. We took 'em to have the straps repaired; he could do anything, put a bed on a cart, build anything but he liked to drink. He'd go t' th' Waterworks or th' Black Horse at Endon. He had a bike that he called Brenda, he talked to it. He'd fall off it, then he'd coss a bit, collect his self and start again.

When I got married we started farming at Gibraltar Farm, then Broadmeadows came up for rent; dad wanted my brother to go to Gibraltar and us to go to Broadmeadows. It was a big mistake; the previous tenants had the farm taken off them, the War Ag had got it and you had to do as they wanted which cost a lot of money. We had to put a lot of lime on and they sent crawler tractors in to plough which ploughed too deeply and fetched the subsoil up so the clay was on the top and spoilt the land. One 40 acre field was ruined and there were no subsidies then. The War Ag didn't know about farming and messed it all up and if you didn't do as they wanted, you were turned off.

Dick, Doris and Hazel at Gibraltar.

Ena Fryer

My late husband, Roy Fryer came from Royal Cottage, Troughstones, Biddulph Park. I came from Park Mount Farm, Macclesfield. We met at a dance at Eaton and were married at Gawsworth Church and went to live at Little Knowles, Top Road, Biddulph Moor. We had a few cattle and he worked at Big Fenton, Buglawton for George Moss. He also worked at Green Tree, Rudyard for Charlie Woodward for a while and Bill Gibson's at Rushton, but there was no time off except on a Sunday. It was said that lads went home to have their shirts washed then.

So quite a few of the lads from Biddulph Moor decided to give their farm jobs up and go to work in the pit, so that they had more time off to do work at home and probably more money too.

Then in 1958, this place, Park House came up for sale with 55 acres and we went to the auction. It didn't reach the reserve, so the vendors gave it out that they would loan three quarters of the money if the buyer could put up one quarter. Still nobody bid, so I knocked Roy's knee, *'Let's see if they'll rent it to us.'* So we went up, but they wouldn't, but they would lend us the money, they wanted £4,000. So we said we'd have it and then we came home and started worrying.

Park House Farm.

We'd only got six cattle of sorts, so we let the ground out at first to get some money in and Roy worked in the pit - the Black Bull at Biddulph and on Saturday nights he went delivering eggs for Marjorie Dean at Timbersbrook. He milked the cows before he went to work or else I did them and we built up slowly. He was glad to give up getting coal at the pit, he hated it.

I've been here now for 50 years and got on so well with the local people; they're like my family - I've enjoyed it so much.

George Bailey, roadman, and John Fryer.

John Hawkins and
John Fryer.

Roy Fryer.

George Harrison,
Horton postman.

Tom Heath

When we lived at Bradshaw, Fanny Goodwin kept the Crown Inn at Horton; she kept it herself and had big collie dogs. My brother Jack had to fetch drinking water for her - 6 buckets from a well down Hall meadow. She always gave him a pint of ale and some sandwiches. If I had to do it, she gave me a cup of tea; she never gave me any ale. She fetched it out of barrels in a jug. There was no electric, just oil lamps and she had long clothes, they dragged on the floor. She used to walk from the Crown to Leek; she wouldn't use a bus and wouldn't tread on tarmac - that was the Devil.

I remember in wartime at Great Longsdon, a 500lb bomb dropped one night in Ram Field. I found the cap and plate the next morning. It had been a bad night and the cows had been sheltering at the top of the meadow under the hedge instead of around the field where it would have got them. There was a hencote in the field and shrapnel went straight through it above the hens' heads - they must have ducked - and it sliced thorns off in the hedge behind.

I first started doing grave digging for Sigleys undertakers helping Joe Billinge out; he was grave digger at Longsdon in the 1950s. There were one or two to start with, then as the old grave diggers gave up, I took over.

They asked me to do one at Endon, I had 22 barrowful of soil to wheel away. I had to brick it; line it with bricks after concreting the bottom - it was a vault. That took a day or two. Joe Fox said he couldn't do it, he was grave digger there. While I was doing that, Sigleys rang up about another funeral at Endon. I'm down there so I said, *'Which one is it, I can open it.'* So they rang the vicar who said, *'You'll have to see Joe Fox first.'* Who then said, *'I'll do that.'* It was only an opening. So I told the vicar what he could do and he didn't like it. After that no matter how small the job, he rang me up to do it and old Joe finished,

I once dug another out at Endon and they were supposed be letting me know when the funeral was, so I could go and fill it in. But they never let me know anything. I was going to Bagnall, so I thought I'd ring up to see what was happening. The vicar said, *'Oh, that's gone.'* 'Gone when?' 'I think it was Tuesday.' 'Well, nobody told me nowt about it.' He said, *'I thought it was funny I'd never seen you standing about.'* It'd been left open till after the weekend, just planks pulled over it.

My brother Dick nearly got buried at Endon; he sometimes helped me. It was an opening and he saw the grave stone moving. I said, *'You'd better get out quick!'* and we put a rope round it and tied it to one behind. When I finished, I was digging at 17 churches; including Onecote, Dilhorne, Waterfall, Rushton, Bosley, Horton, Endon, Bagnall, Cheddleton, Ipstones, Wetley Rocks, Cauldon, Calton, Warslow, Forsbrook, Longsdon, Butterton, Grindon. Cauldon and Calton were the worst, on the limestone and very hard work. I hired a Kango and generator; before that it was crowbar and sledgehammer. Rushton is on stone as well but softer sandstone. Some you could dig out in a couple of hours, most take a day, some longer. I got paid 50 bob at start. I finished in 1988, it was £30 then for a new one, openings were less. I used do about 100 a year, so after more than 30 years, I've buried a lot of folks.

We had the job to move the remains from Mount Pleasant Chapel graveyard when that was demolished and they were re-buried in Leek Cemetery. That was with Dick and my son Basil. Peter Howlett and Reg Hill also helped me at times.

A story I was told, the postman at Rushton was walking through the churchyard early one morning on his way to work. Arthur Knowles was digging a grave; he'd got a lamp and was just coming up the ladder out of the hole chuntering to himself. The postman seen him, ran like Hell and did'ner stop till he got down Rushton.

Jim Finney

When war broke out, I joined the Home Guard at Longsdon. The headquarters were at the Memorial Hall and quite a lot of men came out of Leek as well. So I was used to marching and arms drill when I joined the RA Ordnance Corps. We were looking after ammunition, doing essential work moving it about and keeping safe storage.

Jim

I went to Worksop where we were working with large artillery shells; there was no picking them up, they were too big. Then onto another ammunition dump near to Malton before being shipped out from Glasgow on a troop ship.

We moved out one night and met up with a convoy and made off around the top end of Ireland into the Atlantic into the middle of a gale. The ship was in the bottom and you could see a towering mountain of water - quite an experience! I was sick but not scared; I thought we were in good hands.

Every square inch of space was used, you even slept under the tables in the dining room besides sleeping on top of them, there were so many troops on those ships.

We ended up putting foot to shore in Morocco. We were attached to the American 5th Army and went down Algeria and Tunisia squashing the Germans after El Alamein. It was known as Operation Torch and timed to meet the Jerrys coming from the East. We were looking after our own men with ammunition and known as AAD - Advanced Ammunition Depot. The loaded lorries were carried over on barges and convoys stretched as far as the eye could see. We were lucky, rarely under fire. I was out there for $2^{1}/_{2}$ years; it was all top secret at the start; my girlfriend, Gladys didn't know where I was, although we did manage to correspond.

Seminary in Italy where we were billeted in 1943.

From Tunisia, I went to Sicily and then Southern Italy. I got on well with the Italians and picked the language up. I saw the snow line on Vesuvius.

I came back home in 1945, apart from one or two leaves, I'd been away since July 1942. We were married in 1946.

Finney family.

Reg Barber

I was born in June 1916. I went to Longsdon School; there were a lot of children there then. We marched into school, everything was strict; the roll was called. There were three teachers; Mr Stewart was head, then there was Miss Robinson and Miss Lee who lodged at Stackstones.

My dad, Arthur Barber was fiery tempered and he used to drink a lot at the Waterworks. He lived at the Shrubs down Sutherland Road and was a boot and shoemaker and a postman for a while. He was very good at his work; I used to help hammer the leather. A traveller came round and took the order for leather then my father fetched it from Booths in Leek. It came in a 'bend', a sheet which was rolled up and tied with string. Then he cut out what he wanted. My grandfather was a shoemaker and father had learned from him.

We did as we were told, there were 7 of us, but we lost our home and we were split up and I never knew some of my family until recent years. I went to live with an aunt and uncle at Stanley Bank; I left school at 14 and took newspapers for Andy Dale at Endon. Mr Haig owned the Paper Mill at Cheddleton and the family lived at Longsdon. They were good folks to work for, I did some gardening for them and Mr Haig bought me a bicycle with a carrier on the front so that they could have newspapers delivered.

The papers came on the train to Endon and we loaded a 2ft 6in parcel onto the bike carrier, it was as much as I could hold, a helluva weight. I'd catch hold of wagons for a pull when we came to a hill; if they saw me, they'd slow down and I'd catch hold. I went from Clay Lake to the bottom of Ladderedge delivering papers.

When I was 15 I also went loading coal at the pits filling a $3^1/_2$ ton wagon out of a truck, shovelling through the little doors, loading coal all day; I could shovel both ways. That work was for Arthur Simmonds, coalman on Ladderedge.

I also remember the old brick works on Ladderedge and the relics of the gin rings where they used to press the bricks.

Hilda Barber

I lived at Baddeley Green and when I was18 I met Reg when we went dancing up at Bagnall Post Office. Sixpence it cost and you had a biscuit, a cup of coffee and a nights dancing for that. A chap named Albert Brown taught us different dances.

Reg was in haulage then for Harvey from Endon; then he volunteered and went in the Forces; he became a mechanic in the RAF. We got married and when he came out he was working for a chap named Hails at Baddeley Green doing coal in between taking his papers for Andy Dale who then sold us this area newspaper business.

We looked everywhere for somewhere to move to, then Garnet Shufflebotham persuaded his relations, the Miss Myatts to let us rent a room in their house for a shop. They lived near to the pub at the top of Sutherland road and he thought it was a good idea for us to have premises in Longsdon for a newsagents.

Then we bought this cottage on the crossroads, Henshaw Brow. But after a while the Miss Myatts wanted us to move so Biddy Walker from the opposite side said would we like a room in her house which she didn't use. They were a musical family and there were grand pianos in the room that we turned into the shop. After a while they decided to move and offered us the house to buy, which we did.

Harry and Tom
Wooliscroft of
Harracles Hall
going to
Longsdon School

We built the business up; Reg went round the area with orders and newspapers. We took people on and had three vans which travelled round full of groceries - Longsdon, Horton, Gratton, Ladderedge. Travellers came on a Wednesday; that was closing day and Reg saw them then and the produce was delivered afterwards. Leslie Kirk worked for us. Mr Kershaw also came to drive one of the vans and work in the shop, he could bone the bacon. We sold bread, brushes, wallpaper, paint, groceries, everything. Reg would work all night if he could have - if someone wanted a box of matches, he would have dropped everything and gone to them, he was happy to serve people.

It was a good business until the supermarkets opened. I've dealt with some lovely people over the years who are still my friends. There were awkward ones as well, but that's business.

Julie Stubbs, Longsdon Rose Queen 1968.

View of Longsdon church and Stanlow.

Longsdon School dinner ladies. Back: Mrs Beech,
Mrs Barber, Front: Mrs Addison, Mrs Ford.

Ted Messham

Grandad, Edgar Bennison and his wife Annie moved to Blackwood Hall where he farmed and did some gamekeeping. He then moved to Fields Villa, Gratton Lane, where I was born. He farmed there and sold fruit and veg on a stall in Hanley Market.

He also collected eggs from surrounding farms for North Staffordshire Egg Producers in Hanley. I once went with him as a small boy. On the back seat of the car was the egg crate; one side was full of eggs and in the other was a broody hen. He had to brake suddenly and I remember being covered in broken eggs and having a broody hen flapping round in the car.

Blackwood Hall.

Right: Snow ridding Gratton Lane near Fields Villa. Grandad Bennison, Sid, etc.

Grandad and Ma Sims going milking.

Edgar Bennison of Fields Villa, shearing at Gate House Farm, Endon 1920s.

Above: Joan Bennison feeding turkeys.
Left: Margaret & Spencer Colley, Gratton Lane.

Right: Endon Mill, just
in Horton parish, which
was demolished in the
mid-1930s.

Below: First tractor in
the district - Harry
Brown of Blackwood
Hall Farm. Returning
from Endon after taking
the milk 1940.

Clockwise from top left:
1. Grandad William Sims with Reg Sims, Blackwood Hill Farm.
2. Brenda and Verona Bennison, Blackwood Hall.
3. Joan Bennison at Villa Farm.
4. Grandad Bennison's car, with Joan and Brenda.

Mr Moss, Blackwood Grange about 1960.

Irene & Eric Moss, Blackwood Grange
with Ted Messham.

Norman Hall

I was born at Blackwood Grange in January 1918. It was 140 acres which my parents rented from Colonel Dobson of Seighford Hall near to Stafford. He owned most of Blackwood at that time.

Father died in 1929 and it was then too much for mother to manage even with the help of my brother Joe who was 10 years older than me. So we had to push Sims out of the bottom place, Blackwood Hill and farm it - we could manage 56 acres better. It was hand-milking then and we kept free range hens, there were hencotes all over the place. You had to go round them in the different fields twice a day to feed them and collect the eggs. That was before the days of intensive hen farming with hundreds kept in lofts and sheds.

Norman Hall in Home Guard uniform
at Blackwood Hill, 1944.

We kept about 24 milking cows in shippons of 5 or 6 tied by the neck, cleaned out with a wheelbarrow and fed through foddering or fothering holes out of the fotherbin. The loose hay was in the loft above and dropped down through a hole into the fotherbin.

I suppose it was a privilege living at Blackwood, we felt a bit more upper class than Lask Edge or Mow Cop. The land joined up to Blackwood Hall, part of which was rented to Edgar Bennison for a while. He ran a stall on Hanley Market and used to buy our eggs which he used to pick up in a big car. He would do butchering as well and used to kill and cut up for local people.

I started attending Gratton Chapel when I was 2½ and started playing the organ for the Sunday school later. I picked up the elementary principles of playing the piano when Mrs Morley from Endon Mill was giving my sister Winnie lessons. Then I had some lessons from my second cousin, William Robert Bailey who played the organ at Hill Top chapel. I had 18 months lessons on the American organ, then I was going to go onto the pipe organ but couldn't get very far on that because there was hardly any practice. I could play the organ at Hill Top free of charge but you had to pay two lads to blow it for you. It was only 3d an hour but when you were farming you had to do your practice at night after you'd done your share of milking. That meant going to cottage no.1 for a key, cottage no.2 for a boy and cottage no.3 for another boy. If it was dark you had to light the lamps. It only took one boy at a time to blow but you couldn't have one without the other - they were the blowers.

In the 1930s, the Clowes family from Blackwood House farm were a musical family at Gratton chapel, Martha was a good soloist, and Katie, and Mr Clowes was choirmaster. We used to borrow people from Endon, Biddulph Moor and Lask Edge and have a good choir for harvest or anniversary to sing anthems together.

I got into playing for chapel services and have played for special services at Longsdon, Endon, Lask Edge and at Kinsey Street and Mossley at Congleton. I have played the organ for the last ten years at Wetley Rocks too. It has been a lifelong love of mine. In 1986 I was given permission to play the organ at Westminster Central Hall for my own amusement - a great thrill.

The Hall family at
Stoneywood farm,
Endon c.1880.

Standing: Bill Bosson.
Sitting centre:
Jacob Hall.

Right:
Hannah & Ginny Hall.

Joseph and Ruth Hall at
Blackwood Grange,
1928, with their children
Charles, Winnie, Joe,
Annie and Norman.

Jake Hall's first motor
lorry - a 1922 Fiat.

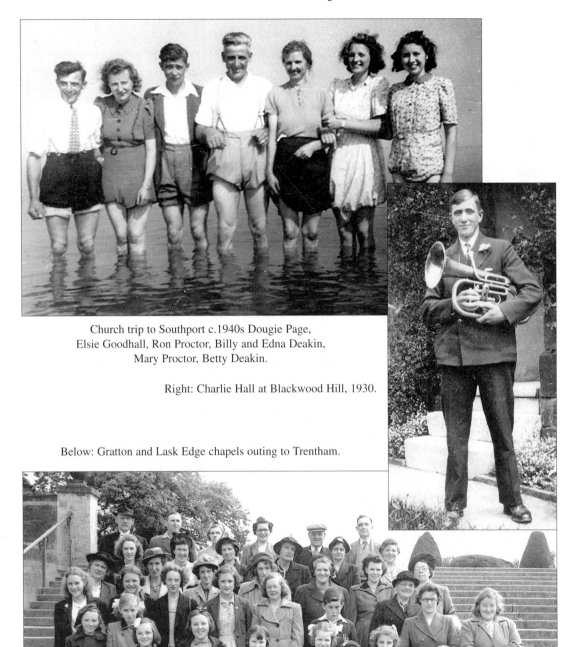

Church trip to Southport c.1940s Dougie Page,
Elsie Goodhall, Ron Proctor, Billy and Edna Deakin,
Mary Proctor, Betty Deakin.

Right: Charlie Hall at Blackwood Hill, 1930.

Below: Gratton and Lask Edge chapels outing to Trentham.

Alan Williamson

Wallgrange has always been a very important place with regards to water supply. There's an old well there that goes back certainly to Roman times, and possibly much earlier than that, called St Coenas Well. Early in the 1800s people realised what a valuable source of water this could be for the then growing conurbations of the Pottery Towns. With the river Churnet and its major tributary the Endon Brook meeting within a few hundred yards of this well, there was obviously a lot of water to be tapped there if anyone could devise a means of pumping it out and getting it to these industrial towns where it was needed.

What they decided to do eventually was to sink a well and put in a steam pump and this scheme went ahead in the late 1840s. They put together what became the Staffordshire Potteries Water Board with people like the Duke of Sutherland and maybe the Wedgwoods, Spodes and others in pottery manufacture amongst the directors to get the capital together for the scheme.

The construction of this pumping station was quite an undertaking because Wallgrange was then a remote part; there was no railway then in the Churnet or Endon valley and anything needed had to be provided locally or brought in on the canal. At that time in the 1840s the real experts in this country in pumping were the Cornishmen and the firm down in Cornwall who made the engine, the pump and the boiler had to construct all this heavy machinery, then load it on a boat and sail around Lands End and up around Wales and Holyhead to get to Liverpool. Then it had to be stripped

down enough to enable it to be transported in a narrowboat and so from Liverpool it was brought along the Trent and Mersey canal and then up the Caldon branch and then up the Leek Arm of the canal and unloaded at Wallgrange.

Also when you think that communication was probably then by post or horseback, what a tremendous undertaking for the transactions and specifications etc.

When the first equipment was brought, the boat was caught in a storm off Holyhead and was sunk and the gear and 18 months work went to the bottom of the Irish Sea. However, at the second attempt, the equipment arrived safely. It was then assembled but they realised that this advanced

Wallgrange Pumping Station.
Davenport on the left,
Stafford on the right.

technology, as it was then, was beyond any local persons understanding and needed proper care and maintenance. So they managed to persuade the man who had overseen the erection of the equipment, and who had come from Cornwall, to bring his family up and a house was built for him to stay there and look after the job. Several generations of the family carried on this job and in Longsdon Memorial hall, one is recorded as being killed in the first war.

Betty Simpson

I was born at The Waterworks, Wallgrange also known as Wallgrange pumping station. My father was James Bunting, known as Jim; he was the manager - the engineer - and he supervised it all. It was a big business then, all run by steam and employed a lot of men. There were four men on a shift, that was 12 men stokers and engine men that worked on the upper floors and 4 other men did the outside work.

There were 2 pumphouses, six fires and boilers - the boilers were Cornish, I remember it being written on them. It was all very powerful; the water was pumped right through to Birches Head in the Potteries. The rods and pipes used to go right up three storeys and there was a great beam. People came from all over the place to see it; it was beautifully kept, cleaned and oiled and all the inside walls were whitewashed. There were big clocks which regulated the steam and if anything went wrong in the night, they'd fetch father out.

The coal came on barges pulled by horses and they used to come down onto the gardens while the boats were being unloaded to have something to eat. The coal was dropped into a pit and then the men would wheel it in for stoking up - it stood in piles by the engine house.

They used to empty all the coal and then we children used to get on the barges and ride with them while they went to turn round at Tunnel Pool. The lady on one boat used to fry liver and onions and we sat in the cabin and ate it. They came two or three times a week, it used a lot of coal.

When I look back on it, it was lovely, the canals were busy, boats going to Boltons at Froghall and Brittains Paper

Wallgrange- the manager's house with the boardroom in the middle.

The Wallgrange brickworks.

Mill on the bottom canal. The boatees were very friendly. The brickworks wasn't far away - I remember them quarrying the marl and seeing the lorries carting the bricks away. And of course the mental hospital was nearby and a lot of people who lived in the village worked there and came through the grounds to go to work across the canal. They ran a special train to bring visitors to the hospital on a Sunday afternoon from the Potteries.

The waterworks was run by Staffordshire Potteries Water Board and there was a board of directors who used to come out and visit and a board room was attached between the houses where they met every year. When I lay in bed at night, I could hear it pumping. It wasn't a big noise, more of a clank. It all went when it became powered by electric.

There were six children in our family, we used to play like mad - paddle in the brook, ride on the barges, children from the village came down and we played rounders and cricket on the grass. Fred Turner, the Halls from Wood Road, Madge, Jack and Joyce. When the weather was bad, we were stuck in and in winter father would light a big fire in the board room so all us children could go in there and play. We used to put a net across the middle and bat a ball across it.

We were banned from Deep Haye because it was too dangerous but when father went up to register things, we went with him.

On a summer Sunday it was very busy around home; we used to picnic in the garden and relatives and cousins often came. One was a great pal; Helen, but we always called her Nell. Her brother won a scholarship to Oxford and became a Don. He took Holy Orders and became chaplain to St Stephens House and taught Latin, Hebrew, Greek and English. When they dug up the Dead Sea Scrolls, he was sent out there to help decipher them. When he came back, he wasn't happy and didn't go back to Oxford. He took to the area around Gawsworth and became vicar there. Rev Henry Saunders, known as Harry. He was part of my childhood at Wallgrange.

The war came and changed everything - everything was blacked out and the Home Guard did duty at the Waterworks; some men were always on guard at night, even father.

When the war ended, I joined the Amateur Dramatic Society. I always went to church and I sang in the choir. I still support the village functions. I remember the Rev Herbert Barton; I acted and sang with him. He was big and lovely and had a beautiful singing voice, he'd been a singer with the BBC.

Left to right:
Jeanette Pember,
Roy Hewson,
Doris Jeffrey,
Herbert Barton,
Margaret and
Peter Hall.

George Beswick

My father, Thomas Beswick came from Biddulph, his family before him had come from Flash. He was a gamekeeper for Munroes at Fairview, Rudyard. My mother, Lily Rose Gibson, was a tailoress; she made all our clothes, stockings and everything. She was from a well-to-do family; her father, Thomas Gibson was a property dealer. Father bought 15 farms at Much Wenlock for grandad; 11 one night at an auction. We should have gone to one of these farms; we lived at Horse Pastures and dad gave in his notice to go but grandad sold it over his head. So he bought 42 acres of ley ground at Horton. There was just a shed on it that cattle could go in and he built Brownslow farmhouse there in 1921.

He went over the hedge and got the stone out of the next field. Dan Lancaster was the builder. I used to walk with dad from Biddulph to spend the day getting stone out; I'd only be about 6 and I only remember it in nice weather. I remember one day around then going for a row with him across Rudyard Lake. We were going across the middle of the lake, as wide as anywhere and this stoat was swimming across in the middle of the lake. Dad got his belt off and picked it up into the boat and let it go when we got to the side. I've never forgotten it.

I was born in 1913; there were 9 of us but one girl died when she was 8. So I was left with 3 brothers and 4 sisters, Bill, Tom and Frank, Phyllis, Mabel, Flossie and Lily. Mother died when I was 12. There was no water or electricity at the house, just a well which you fetched water from in a bucket. The stock had to be turned out to a pond and I've carted hundreds of gallons of water from Sam Turnocks at Coneygreave. I used to shoot a lot of rabbits and sell them in Rudyard or Leek for half a crown in winter and a shilling in summer. I skinned 20 a week for the Miners' Home in Rudyard. I had to shoot a lot of pigeons too; there were always a lot in the corn. My wife, Dora made a lovely pigeon pie.

Tom Beswick 1948.

Phyllis and George at Dairy House 1928.

George at Brownslow
early 1930s.

Back: George, Dora,---, Phillip
Front: Winifred, ---

Below:
Percy Williamson returning
from Horton Hay,
early 1920s.

In wartime I'd got a black market pig hanging up in the coal house and Eric Gaskill turned up. He worked for Joe Day at Taylors Barn and he'd been ploughing and got his pair of horses fast in the brook and couldn't get them out himself. Luckily he didn't see anything.

I used to make bacon - salt it for 10 days, then get it into the house, soft and roll it very tight so there was no air in it, put string round it and hang the sides of bacon up to dry. The pigs were big; 14-15 score (about 300lbs). My brother Tom did a lot of pig killing; he was licensed. We also made black puddings in basins - boiled it like Christmas puddings. Dad did some butchering; he made sausages and had a stall on Hanley market. Mr Smith, who lived on Biddulph Moor used to come along at the end of the day on a Saturday and want a great ruck of sausage for a shilling - '*10 lb for a bob!*' He wanted to beg what was left. Dad got ready for him one day; he got nothing but fat and pumped it into these sausage skins and Mr Smith took them. The next week he came back and all he could say was, '*Nay! What about them sausage?*'

We grew potatoes and sold them; at potato picking time children came from Rudyard to help. Dora insisted on giving everyone a proper dinner - there could be 24 of us. We also grew other crops; year after year I won first prize for the best crop of kale in Leek and District. It was taller than me; we had to cut it and cart it to the yard, then carry it into the shed for the cattle, often wet and frozen.

I've grown turnips weighing 23lbs each and 8lb beetroots. The secret is a good muckcart. We grew cow cabbage, they are very large. I once saw 5 on a trailer in Uttoxeter market and they filled it, they were that big. One year mushrooms grew under the cabbage in the plough field, loads and loads. The kids went hawking them round the caravan site in Rudyard.

One family, the Taylors from the Potteries, used to come for eggs, and their boys, Alf and Derek and their friend John Harvey started coming camping; they'd be about 11. I used to send them to Endon Smithy with the horses to be shod. One morning I altered their clock so that they thought they were late. They got to Endon on the horses backs and said to Charlie Perkin, '*We're getting hungry, we haven't had dinner yet.*' He replied, '*I anner 'ad my breakfast yet!*'

They loved coming and came every weekend. Mr Taylor bought a van and dropped it in a little valley which the boys came and lived in, you couldn't see it. John was at Hanley High School but wanted to come and work for us. But to leave at 15, his mother had to pay; his father worked in the pit. He begged her to let him leave and eventually persuaded her. He worked for us for 11 years.

I bought Brownslow when dad died in 1949 and in 1960 bought the neighbouring farm, Birch Trees. Mr Dickenson came every day to try and get me to buy it. I took over March 25th and there were 40 acres of corn planted which we had to get with a binder. I had my teeth out then as well. Someone rang while I was at the dentist wanting to buy it, but Dora never told me; she thought I might have sold it again for a bit of profit; but I wouldn't have sold it on any footing.

We also kept 500 hens - Rhode Island Red hens with Sussex cockerels and sold eggs for hatching. So every hen had to be caught for blood testing twice a year. They were all free range, 11 hencotes the length of the ground. I mixed wet corn for them - flaked maize and thirds mixed with hot water. I carried bags of that to them when I let them out and they had grain at night. A lady from the ministry came and we had to black the windows out so that we could catch the hens, then we took a dab of blood from under their wing and put it on a plate, then let the hen go outside. The eggs made 8s a doz for hatching when we got 4s a doz from the packing station

I had my first baler, a Massey Harris 701 with an engine on in 1958. I've always enjoyed baling and have done it right up until 2006 and still hope to do a bit more.

Ron Heath

When we were children at Great Longsdon, we had 500 fruit trees, apples, plums, damsons, red and black currants and gooseberries. We cut them back every year and set the cuttings to make more. We all had to help pick and sell; there were always plenty of customers. As we got older we liked to go out on a Saturday night and sometimes dad would say, *'No going out tonight, we'en got all this fruit pickin'; it'll be droppin' off else.'* So we had to wait till the next weekend. Same as haymaking time, he'd say, *'We've got to get the hay, it'll be raining tomorrow.'* And he was usually right.

I used to cut a lot of sticks and logs, I'd get half a crown for a bag of logs and 5 shillings for sticks. Mum used to buy new clog soles and tips on a Wednesday, take the old ones off at night, clog 'em and they'd be ready for school the next morning. She must have worked hours. The wooden soles were joined to the leather uppers with welting which had to be nailed on all round.

Doris Heath

We followed Dick and Doris to Gibraltar Farm after we got married. We had a mixed herd of cows and then went in for Guernseys; we had a market for the milk - Gold Top Channel Island milk. We bottled it all from 33 cows and sold it to Mountside Dairies. They used to pay us every month with a cheque. One

At Gibraltar Farm.
Robert and Ron Heath.

Left: Doris bottling the milk.

month we didn't get the money, so after a week or two, Ron said to Bill Plant, the bookkeeper, *'We haven't had the cheque yet.'* He replied, *'Well, I know I posted it to you; I'll give you another, it'll turn up somewhere.'* After several weeks passed, it came one morning in the post. The address on it was R W Heath, Gibraltar. Written on it was *'Not Known On The Rock.'* It had been to the Rock of Gibraltar.

Margaret Woolley

I was born at Park House Farm, Horton. I remember when my mother had my twin brothers, Dr Miller came and delivered them; he was young and newly passed out and had come to practice in Biddulph. He'd been up with mother all night and next morning he came and had a pillow fight with us girls in the bedroom.

When my father, Arthur Heath was at Horton School, he won a prize in a national competition for scale drawing. The headmaster was over the moon because it had come to a little school like Horton. Dad told us that when he went to the hiring fair in Leek market place he said he was a year older than he was and he went to work for John Knight at Great Longsdon. He had 50 shillings for a years work and he bought a pair of boots to work in with the money.

His mother, Annie, used to nurse people, deliver babies and lay people out. She had flat irons, polishing irons and little tiny irons; I remember seeing them kept in a cupboard at Park House. She used to do laundry and starch shirt collars and things for gentry people as well.

One night she'd been looking after someone who was ill at Bond House and she was walking back through the fields to White Cottage, where they lived. She could hear a swishing noise and when the moon came out from behind a cloud, she could see a horde of rats; so she stood still and they went past. It was said if you kicked or upset them, they would attack you.

When we were scuffling potatoes, turnips or mangolds, I had to lead the horse and I couldn't go fast enough with my wellies on, so I kicked them off and ran barefoot, being careful the horse didn't tread on me. I once remember a terrible storm, I've never known another as bad; it lasted all day, lightning was dropping in the yard all the time. Dad was carrying sheets of zinc across the yard to cover a load of hay and the lightning kept turning him round. Len Bailey, a neighbour said, *'Leave off Arthur, you'll be getting killed.'* When they let the horse off the wagon it went into a corner of the yard where it smashed a gate and jumped another one and got away. Neighbours said they saw a ball of fire coming down the fields and went in our building; the roof was ripped off and tiles landed 20 yards away at the back door of the house. Mr Leech, the schoolmaster said afterwards, 'There are 3 children in school this morning who are lucky to be alive. A man called Ned Heath was killed on the top road.

We had lots of hencotes and in wartime dad fixed one up for three Polish refugees to live in, one was called Minke and another Laurence. He used to ask mum to play the organ and he would sing 'The Holy City' in broken English. They didn't stop long because someone told of dad and they were going to make him pay rates on it.

When mother had the twins, she couldn't help as much outside, so dad got a water lift in the dairy and two milk units which ran off an

Ready to shoot rats at Park House.
L-R: Arthur Heath, Bill Stonier, Frank Brown.

engine. Then when we left school and were big enough to milk he sold them and we had to go back to hand-milking and hand pumping the water. There was a well in the yard and we pumped the water into a big tank which fed the water bowls.

Dad was often called upon to help neighbours out. He was good at vetting animals and had a vet book which he kept on a beam in the barn. One neighbour even used to get a ladder up to his bedroom window to knock dad up if he wanted help to calve a cow. Dad was one of the few people to keep a bull then and quite a few people brought their cows up to be served.

Alice and Arthur. Florrie, Norah and Margaret.

Margaret.

Family group of Heaths and Bowyers at Park House.

Bert Clews

My grandfather, Herbert Clews came to Boot Hall as a tenant in 1901. It was part of the Horton Hall estate along with New House Farm, where Mellors were, Townsend and Bond House. Then the farms were sold off and the tenants had the chance to buy.

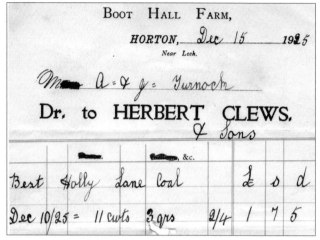

BOOT HALL FARM,

HORTON, *Dec 15* 1925

Near Leek.

M— A. & y. *Turnock*

Dr. to HERBERT CLEWS.
& Sons

		&c.	£	s	d
Best Holly Lane Coal					
Dec 10/25 = 11 cwts 3 qrs		2/4	1	7	6

Grandfather did some horse-dealing, pig-killing and delivered coal to houses and farms in the area. The lads would fetch it from Rudyard Station - unload it out of the trucks, shovel it into their carts, then weigh it on the weighbridge there and deliver it. There were 11 children and their mother died aged 36.

I was born at Boot Hall in 1925. Mrs Hall was at Horton Hall then, living on her own, her husband had died. I think they belonged to Brough, Nicholson and Hall and had mills in Leek.

At one time then, there were 11 of us living at Boot Hall. Sydney, a cousin from Brookhouse was reared with us. His mother died when he was a fortnight old and so they brought him up for my mother and Aunt Mary to rear; he was like another brother to me.

The milk went to London on the train from Rudyard station. In summertime they used to send word to keep your milk at home for so many days a week; they didn't want it. So we had to make butter and cheese. There were big presses in the kitchen and the cheeses were stored on the bedroom floor over the living room; it was known as the cheese room. They were big cheeses. There were 2 cast iron presses and a big wooden one.

The milk was put in a big round vat, the rennet was put in and it was stirred and then put in a big wooden box which caught the whey. A board was put on and screwed down and the whey ran out of the front and was caught. That was the first pressing, then we put cloths in the metal moulds, filled them with the curds and they went into the iron presses and were screwed down.

There were big flat pitcher pans to put the milk in for butter making. It was left to settle, then the cream was

Clews family. Albert, William, Arthur, Mary, Herbert, Jessie, Fred.

Aunty Jessie and Aunty
Mary at Boot Hall 1930.

Townsend, Horton -
fetching the cows back to
Boot Hall 1930

Boot Hall cornfield

skimmed off. They stood on the stillages in the pantry which faced north so it didn't get the sun.

When there were plenty of eggs, they were stored in deep earthenware steins in what we called si-glass (isinglass). They were used to bake with in winter when the hens weren't laying.

We milked 35 to 40 cows, grew corn, swedes, mangolds, cabbage and potatoes. Father used to take a load of potatoes in hundredweight Hessian sacks to the Potteries with 2 horses in a dray. He told me when they met steam wagons on the road, the horses really pranced about and he had to really stick hold of them. When he'd unloaded somewhere in Hanley, he'd go to Cliff's Brewery and load his dray up with horse manure and bring that back.

I remember Mr Bradley who used to be at Townsend was a roadman paid by the council. He cleaned the ditches out, cut the grass verges with a badging hook, cleaned the gutters out and swept up.

Moss road wasn't open then; farmers on the Horton estate had to mend it and other roads. They had to get so many loads of stone out of Cliff Wood up at Blackwood House. So many loads a day and break it and mend the roads.

I can remember Mellors having a big gate outside New House and they kept it locked. The gate and road belonged to them and if you wanted to go down with a horse and cart you had to go to them and pay a shilling, which was a lot then and they'd unlock the gate. There was another gate at Lyme House end and also little gates on the side, so you could get through with a riding horse and not have to pay. Then some farmers kept pressing the council to buy the road off Mellors and eventually they agreed to sell it and it became a public road, now known as Tollgate Road.

Mellors also had Tollgate Cottage where the bridleway goes in down the fields and over the old stone bridge and out at Blue Gates. There was a big gate and a small gate there, always painted blue in my time. Between Tollgate Cottage and Horton Hall was Stock Well and an old lane known as Butchers lane went in; a right of way to a field belonging to Boot Hall and fields belonging to Mellors, we had to fetch water from the well in a dry time with float and milk churns. Mellors used it too. Jack Edge at Horton Head and Mellors used the watering hole opposite Tollgate Cottage for their cattle.

I remember Maurice Shaw, a solicitor from Leek used to ride through on his horse from Blue Gates and come out up Butchers Lane.

When the war came, there were a lot of us at Boot Hall, so I went working at Pump Farm, Warslow for John Critchlow. That's where I met my wife Olive.

The Watering Hole, Tollgate Cottage is on the left.

John Critchlow, Pump Farm, Warslow.

John Clews and Abel Heath (Blake House).

Heath family at Fields Farm c.1902.

Norah Proctor

I was born at Fern Cottage in 1921; there were four of us, Mary born 1919, Sam in 1922 and Edna in 1927, so we're all now in our 80s. The first thing I remember is some girls' clothes coming from relatives in Leek. I tried on a grey coat; it had a big mother-of-pearl clasp fasten and mother said it would do for school. I wore it for as long as it fitted me.

Dad brought shopping home from Leek on Saturday nights. We had beef for Sunday dinner and often had oranges, sliced and sprinkled with sugar for Sunday tea. He also brought cod liver oil and malt and green Snowfire tablet for winter chaps. We had Copes Pine Balsam for coughs and colds. Copes Chemists used to be on the corner at the bottom of Fountain Street.

I remember grubbing with our fingers for pig nuts which grew in the croft and gathering dry sycamore leaves into corn sacks to use as bedding in the hencotes. I recall mother crocheting a lace edging to stitch onto the window blind. She kept a few plants on a table in the porch and she used to mix hen manure in water to use as a liquid fertilizer. Mary still has her aspidistra; some years ago she gave both me and Edna roots from it, all are still doing well.

Mother, Hannah on the dolly tub, at Fern Cottage

I remember mother fetching water from Gratton Spout by the chapel. It ran slowly and while waiting for the bucket to fill, she was knitting; she used to knit wool vests for us. Edna was in the pram; someone stopped to look at her and said, 'What a bonny baby.'

Gratton Chapel.

Dad was repairing his motor bike one Sunday; he needed it for work the next day. Then he went for a ride on it to check if it was alright. He'd left all his tools in a heap near the little gate to the cottage. That was the day Gratton Chapel singers came! They always came just before the Sunday School Sermons, sang a hymn and collected money. Mother was not very pleased.

Sometimes dad came home in the steam wagon, parked it in the yard overnight and next day went to Whitfield for a load of coal for Tattons. Sutton's bus came from Biddulph through Gratton and Endon and on to Leek. We got on at our gate; mother took butter to sell. She, along with others stood in the Buttermarket at Leek. People also took eggs and dressed poultry.

There was a full chapel for Gratton Sermons and people including mother were standing outside. I've always remembered when we had the tea party the following Saturday, the swing with its wooden seat and thick rope. It hung from the oak tree that is still in the corner of the field, by the finger post, which belonged to Lower House.

We had wooden rain water tubs; they had strips of wood formed into a barrel shape with metal bands to hold them together. After a spell of dry weather, they leaked water until they were thoroughly soaked again and then the water would be black with soot that had been washed from the roof.

I remember Edna being christened. Horton vicar wouldn't do it this particular day because it was the harvest. Mother had prepared all the food so dad went on his motorbike to ask Endon vicar, so she was christened at Endon Church. Dad's cousin, Elsie Wood from Poets Cottage was Godmother. The best tea set was used; it had a pretty border in blue, harebells and grasses.

Sometimes dad would say, 'We'll have a sing-song. He knew many old songs, every word, all the verses and the tunes. Where did he learn all those? We hadn't any music that I can think of.

Air Raid Precautions

It was before the war began in about 1938 that I along with others attended a meeting at Horton Lea School. Then someone came and gave a course of lectures; mostly First Aid - how to stop bleeding and the correct way to apply bandages. Then a large van came and one at a time we entered and were given a whiff of mustard gas, so we would know what it smelled like. Following that we had a written exam. These passed and became ARP Wardens: William Bailey of Halfway House, Joseph Day - Taylors Barn, Abel Heath - Bond House, Stephen Heath - Boosey Lane, Nancy Heath, Stephen's daughter, Edward 'Ted' Lambert, Lea Laughton, Rev. A R Smith, The Vicarage, Norah Wood - The Homestead, Gratton.

Lea Laughton.

When the vicar announced the results he remarked how well the two young ones had done, Nancy and myself. The vicar became Head Warden; it had to be someone with a telephone and he was the only one who had one. Then we were measured for and had uniforms. The men had navy trousers and tunic, cap, overcoat and boots. Mine was

At Fields Farm 1933.

Norah in ARP uniform.

navy serge skirt and jacket, hat, overcoat and shoes. I also had a pale blue blouse and tie.

Later we held one or two sessions to issue gas masks. They had straps and had to be adjusted to fit each person. They were busy sessions; we covered Horton, Horton Hay, Gratton, Blackwood and part of Lask Edge. It was decided to meet regularly in case any fresh instructions came. The meetings were held at Miss Lizzie Hine's at Church View; she always made us very welcome. One of the farmers brought along milk, tea, sugar and biscuits. I remember Miss Hines' beautifully polished range grate with roaring fire and singing kettle and her treasured collection of Coronation and Jubilee mugs which she kept on top of a lovely old chest of drawers.

When the war started, the Head Warden said we had to have an ARP Post and it had to be 'manned'. A garage by the side of the Vicarage became the Post. The men did night duty and the women daytime duty. I only remember Nancy and myself and I'm sure she had a job then too but it wasn't long before she went into the Forces (Women's Army). After a short time we abandoned this; we didn't seem to be doing anything there and we all had work to do. Fortunately we didn't have any wartime incidents in our area. I remember us all in uniform attending Armistice Sunday service at Church.

Sam Wood

I was born in 1922 at Fern Cottage, Gratton. My grandad farmed at Broad Meadows, then went down Monmouthshire and bought a farm down there. My parents were Hannah and Samuel; dad lived in the cottage here and worked for Tattons Mills in Leek. He drove a

Tatton's Burrell steam wagon 1920s. Sam Wood Snr (L), Walter Heath, fireman (far right).

steam wagon and was coming down Cat Tor at Upperhulme to the old mill when the fly wheel split, hitting him on the head and killing him. I can't remember my mother, she died before dad. I remember him saying to me, *'Your mum's gone to Jesus.'* And that stuck in my mind; I thought if dad's gone same place as mother, mother hasn't come back and dad won't come back and I sobbed for a couple of weeks. That's all I can remember; me and Norah went to live at Brookhouse to our aunt's.

There were 6 children at Bond House and I used to go up and play with them. Alan and me used to go round the brooks at night catching trout; we could get 12 to 15, some decent fish. When we'd finished he'd say, 'W*ell, there's six of us children, me dad and mother, Vernon and*

STRUCK BY FLYING METAL.

Gratton Steam Wagon Driver Killed.

A verdict of " Accidental death " was returned at an inquest held by Mr. S. A. H. Burne, District Coroner, and a jury at Leek Town Hall on Saturday afternoon on Samuel Wood, a widower, aged 37, of Yew Tree Villa, Gratton, Endon, who was killed in an accident at Upperhulme on the previous Thursday.

Evidence of identification was given by John James Clewes, of Brook House Farm, Horton, who said Wood was a steam wagon driver employed by Messrs. W. A. Tatton and Co., Ltd., Upperhulme.

FLY-WHEEL BROKE.

Walter Heath, of Smithy Cottage, Gratton, Endon, said that about 5 p.m. on Thursday he was on a steam wagon driven by Wood and loaded with lime. The wagon was returning down a hill at Upperhulme, near the Roaches, in low gear at a very slow speed, probably not more than 3 m.p.h. The vehicle had a foot-brake on the fly-wheel and also a foot-brake on the back wheels, both of which the driver was using. Apparently the back brake must have got worn and was not acting very well and Wood was applying extra pressure on the fly-wheel brake. with the result that the wheel got so warm that it expanded, broke in two and went off with a bang. The flying pieces caught Wood, who fell over on to witness. A portion of the wheel must have struck the water glass, which broke, causing the steam to come out. Witness shut off the steam and water and drew up the wagon by steering it on to the grass verge by the wall which bordered the road. The wagon was not out of control when the wheel broke.

Daisy as work for us; that's 10 and I had to have anything left over 10.'

I had to go church 3 times; morning service, afternoon in the schoolroom and church again at night - a bit much for a child. Mr Whieldon was the best vicar, really respected; in the schoolroom you could hear a pin drop. But then I remember a man committed suicide on the Friday afternoon - we were talking about it at choir practice at night. They'd sent for the vicar to him but then on the Sunday the vicar had a heart attack and died.

One of my first memories is of playing in the lane and I saw two black horses and a carriage draw up outside Gratton Villa, which was known as 'th' hodge', where Rafe Heath lived. I got behind a bush watching; it would be his funeral. He was a gentleman and had a pony and trap. The pony was hard to catch so on a Tuesday he'd get it up into the orchard at the back of the house ready to go to Leek the next day. Jess and Langford Brassington were me dad's mates and Jess told me they'd go and let this pony out and lay it on me dad. Old Rafe would say, 'Samuel, have you let my pony out again!' They were always up to some tricks; they tied Arthur Heath's trap up in a tree once when he wanted to go courting and he couldn't get it down so he had to go on the horses back.

One Friday in 1934 a big snow dropped; it drifted in no time. My relations at The Ashes, Vera and Nelly had to carry the little ones on their backs home from School. A feller named Simcock from Brown Edge used to come round with a pony and flat cart with greengrocery on a Friday and go as far as the Crown at Horton. This day he got as far as Brook House and couldn't get any further so we put the pony and stuff in a building and he stopped with us till Tuesday. I've often thought there were no telephones; they wouldn't have known what had happened to him. On the Tuesday the sun came out, it started melting; he got the pony out and went home.

I can remember the smithy at Gratton; Trevor Goodall was blacksmith; he lived in the little cottage this side, I can just remember him working. On the other side was a loft with steps and they used to keep the iron up there. Then the place where they put the shoes on, that's the shop window now, then this side was where they had the anvil and made the shoes.

I went to work for Fred Cotton at Hurst Farm, Waterhouses. He had a big farm, perhaps 300 acres before the cement works came. There were 20 acres

Jennifer Proctor and Sandra Wood
at The Homestead, Gratton.

of green crop and a lot of cows; he used to cattle deal. We used to go down to Lancasters and Arthur Moss's near Congleton every week and buy about 10 heifers and then farmers came and bought some of them and we kept the leavins. There came a cattle wagon Monday morning with 'em. We did a lot of cattle droving; there were two of us on the farm, me and Alan Goldstraw a while and Eddy Brassington was there a while, then he got married and I had to do the waggoning and everything. It was the 1940s and war was on. Fred was on the War Ag. We had two Italian POWs worked for us and they slept in; I didn't know much Italian, I didn't know if they were cossin' me or what. One was very nice but the other wasn't.

Fred used to go round at night buying cattle off farmers. *'Have you got any barren cows, slips or anything like that?'* then on Thursday morning, after breakfast, he'd take you round same as up Ipstones Edge and Foxt, all round Oakamoor and say, *'There's 5 there, 3 there, 4 there and you'd have to go on your own.'* Ee, I've run my heart out till I couldn't go and you'd finish up with about 40 cattle in the road and come down to the Hurst Farm with them about half past twelve and then have our dinner. Then two of us would walk them to Ashbourne; we'd have about 70 then, a road full and walk them towards Ashbourne and down to Clifton Station, where we put them on the train - box 'em all up ready for the ten past four train. The engine came in and took them down to Market Harborough. There was a fellow down there called Charlie Bury used to buy them. He also came up to Leek Market on a Wednesday. He'd pick me up and take me into Leek with him into Haywood Street, the market was there then.

He'd be buying and I put them into them pens down the side of Haywood street and then when the market was over, he'd get a drover out of the market to help me and I had to take them down to Leek station then and there'd be trucks in waiting. We put them on there - it was a mauling job because each one was individual, I can't remember if we put them on heads all one way; there was a big chock rail in between each one and you had to put them all in a row on the wagons. Push one in, drop a rail in place, then push another in place. They all had horns, but I don't remember getting hurt.

When we were walking to Ashbourne sometimes, the cows were so tired, they'd want to lie down at the side of the main road. One day in particular, we got down to the Queens at bottom of Swinscoe Bank, it was a hot day and some went off for Tattons Mill on the right. They jumped straight in the river Dove and swam round, 3 or 4 of them. I stood on the bridge throwing at them to stop them going underneath; I thought, 'Them are not going to make it to Market Harborough.' But they came out and finished up going with the rest to graze. He didn't take the thin ones; he said they couldn't stand the land down there, it was too good. So we had to keep them a week or two and they went in the next batch. He'd pick one or two out, 'I daren't take that one Fred.'

The biggest menace was when you had a big Yankee convoy; they didn't care about nothing; we didn't have any accidents though.

I was coming down Stoney Lane one morning and there are 28 railway houses in a row and all these old women were leaning over the gates nattering and these cattle wouldn't face them, their pinafores were blowin'. I'd got about 40 and they split up, half jumped over the wall one side, half jumped the wall the other way. So I fetched them back from one side, got them in the road again and they jumped into the next field and I couldn't get them out. Down at the bottom corner it went into a neck so I had to push them into this corner and jump them over the wall and down the road.

I'd sometimes go with Fred buying the cattle on a Saturday night. We went to Lancasters first; we called him Russia. If Fred couldn't buy, he'd say, *'Well, we conna do no good with thee this week, we'll go down the road to Arthur.'* And we'd go and buy 10 from Arthur.

They mostly came from Ireland and the stock did very well going onto the limestone; they were cows the next year. We sold most of them, but kept the worst, milked them and turned them away and they developed into good cows.

We used to keep two shire stallions. One we travelled, towards May time. It was by Edingale Blend, one of Colonel Nicholson's from Highfield Stud. We'd taken a mare there and kept the foal. We called him Cauldon Blend; he was bay with a white blaze and four white legs. Farmers would bring mares while you were having your dinner and you had to go out and cover them. You had to take him round to farms as well, but I got as I didn't want that job. Eddy was at Ipstones at Jack Brindleys one Saturday and the stallion kicked him. I was working in the plough field and Fred came and said, *'Bring them horses; Eddy's bin kicked; you've got go Ipstones and fetch the horse back.'* I said, *'Can't he stop up there for the weekend'* - cos I wanted go out Saturday night you see. But he said no and took me Ipstones and I had finish his round off. Richardsons at Bottom Lane; Harold Salt at Green Gutter and another and I finished at Clowes at Onecote Hall. I'd been working in the plough field all morning, my legs ached so I got on his back and rode him back to Waterhouses and I shouldn't have done, it wasn't allowed; they said you hadn't got control of them. I got to Waterhouses and who should come out of the Reading Room but PC Harvey. He just looked at me. *'What are you doing up there?'* I says, *'Me legs ached.'* He says, *'Gerroff the bugger and walk!'* I said, *'I might as well do th' other bit; yer've seen me now.'* I'll never forget it.

That horse he'd rear up and squeal and lay hold of you if you didn't watch it; he got the boss of Eddy. I put a longer rope and a check chain under his jaw, you couldn't play about with 'em. I've often thought about all those mares in foal after that day and they were all filly foals. Then you went round 3 weeks or a month later and tried them behind a gate to see if they were in foal.

Fred used to deal in all sorts of working horses; if someone had one which ran away, he'd swap it for a quiet one. I've had some bad ones; I remember a black one we had from Common End, Swinscoe; I think it was about 7 years old and had been handled but it was the boss. I got it in the chain harrows; it kicked and went mad, it wouldn't go, it lay down. It was in front of Albert's kitchen window, so I thought I'd better go out of sight, too many spectators here. I went down into a 12 acre meadow out of the way. I put a chain round its neck and hooked another horse onto it. It was so stubborn and nasty, the other horse was holding it; I said, 'Hold up steady.' It wanted to sit down and struggle but within 5 minutes that horse had its nose on top of the others back, it didn't want the chain tightened. Then I put them in together into the chain harrows- that field wanted harrowing, it had been mucked and I did it non stop. It kept kicking but by 10 o'clock we'd finished the field and it was white with sweat.

I took it to the yard and put it in the muck cart and put a rope over its back from one shaft to the other to stop it kicking the front of the cart in. I went round the yard and cleaned all the sheds out with it and that was it - it was the best work horse as I ever had after that.

When the war was on we managed to get a tractor because Fred was on Stafford War Ag. Then we had a government thrashing box and used to go round threshing. We'd go as far as Walter Needhams at Wallgrange; I hated the job, you had to carry about ten gallons of water for the tractor - no anti-freeze then - and your farm work to do as well, stock in them little barns all over the farm. Some of us had to go every day for a while; I tried to get out of it, I'd rather stop with the stock.

Then there'd been a snow and the tractor and tackle were up at Calton Moor. There was a corn stack in the yard and it was all over snow. We got there, started up with petrol and then turned over to TVO to get the tractor warm, clean the riddles out and get the bags on. The farm lads were still doing the cows. Jack Cotton, Fred's brother lived at Forest Farm, Swinscoe, so he came across to help. He got on top and started feeding wet sheaves in and not cutting the bonts and there was not a full team. He hadn't been doing it long when he came down off the box minus his arm; it had been caught and ripped off at the shoulder. That was a shock for us all and that was the end of the thrashing box; we never did any more. Jack was only in hospital for about ten days, he healed up very fast.

One Saturday morning about 62 years ago, Fred said to me, *'You've got a job to do today; get your breakfast and get gone.'* It was to flit Hodgkinsons out of the Yew Tree Inn at Cauldon and take 'em into a house down Earlsway with horse and wagon. I had about three loads - gormers on the back and front, old Mettle in the shafts. I used to go down to the Crown at Waterhouses most nights for a shandy. Mr Chadwick was landlord; he wore a white slop. He says, *'Here, have a look at this paper.'* It was the Manchester Guardian and on the front page was a picture of me and the horse and dray and this load of junk, just like Steptoe - jerrys and all sorts, not covered up with it being a dry day, you could see everything. It said, *'British Portland Cement purchases site for cement works.'*

I went for the army but one of my eyes was no good and they wouldn't have me. I went round nine doctors, starkers, and I went up to the desk for my grade card and said, *'What! You anner puttin' me grade 4?' 'Afraid so.' 'What's up with me?'* He laughed, *'We shall be hard up if we send for you.'* I was a reject!

Mary Cartlidge

I have tried to remember what life was like when we lived at Fern Cottage, Gratton. The cottage was attached to the side of the farm buildings but still nicely situated. It would be similar to many in the area; one living room, two bedrooms, one being over a stable, a pantry and kitchen. We had a coal-fired range with oven and boiler at the side and a rack above and mantelpiece. Mother's well-polished jam kettle always stood on the corner cupboard where medicines, cod liver oil and malt and Virol were kept.

Mary.

The sideboard had drawers below for clothes and glass-fronted cupboard above which held a blue and white tea service and other treasures. There was also a sofa, sewing machine and scrubbed-top table, a cold tiled floor and a pegged rag hearthrug. On the walls were one or two pictures and plates and brass candle sticks were on the mantelpiece. Lighting was by paraffin lamp which was filled and trimmed each day.

The cupboard under the stairs held various useful items - the flat irons, the shoe last on which dad fitted clogs to repair tips. His razor strap which was sometimes used on us! The stairs were scrubbed.

Behind the living room was an area containing the separator. Mother put the milk into this, saved the cream then made butter. Then there was a small damp pantry and the kitchen with dolly peg, tub and mangle and brown sink called slop stone. Outside, a small yard and old fashioned privy. I haven't mentioned water; there was none in the house, it came from a draw well in the orchard or a trough in the yard. We fetched drinking water from the spout opposite the chapel.

I can't remember much about food, just porridge and lobby. We always called mother Mamma; she was always busy sewing and knitting. Norah and I once had knitted coats; gingery brown with moss-stitch fronts and round hats with appliquéd leaves.

At Christmas, stockings were hung up and contained perhaps an apple, orange, nuts and sweets and a book if we were lucky. Norah and I once had dolls. When dad brought home a little puppy, we called him after the one in the weekly Leek paper - Topsy, Tommy and the little dog Tim.

Dad worked for Tattons at Upperhulme, the dye works, where he drove a steam wagon and fetched coal from Chatterley Whitfield Colliery. He also had a motor bike and Mr Walter Heath, who worked with him as the stoker, used a pedal cycle. We had a vegetable garden, a croft for calves and an orchard with apples, damsons and plums. There were hens in the orchard and some along Close Lane. I can't remember how many cattle we had. A cow was always producing milk so we must have had several.

At Horton Lea School, there was head teacher, Mr Leech with his walking stick and cough. In the infants room there was Miss Hine from Horton Post Office. Each room had a round coke stove and sometimes potatoes were placed round to cook. Senior boys carried drinking water from the spring in the lane to Bond House. Norah started school in 1926 and when Sam started we would get him so far down 'Tuncus' Lane then he would run back home and mother would have to take him. Once we were kept off school and went blackberrying for the day.

Gratton Chapel was important in those days; each week there was Sunday school. We were always clean and tidy after our Saturday night bath in the tin bath. Shoes also for Sunday but clogs to school. We had the Annual Sermons; I once sang a solo, an 8 line hymn, *'When the mists have rolled in splendour'*. Each summer we had a tea party; Mrs Hall from Horton Hall came down. We had games and races and scrambled for toffees and nuts in the field opposite Lower House. There was also a swing. We had prizes for good attendance, I still have some.

Mrs Abel Heath was very important; she was our great aunt Annie, grandad's sister and seems to have been the local district nurse and midwife. She helped with sick people, delivered babies and laid out the dead. She was a widow with 5 children.

Our sister Edna was born in 1927; she was tiny and frail and ginger-haired. Children in those days were all breast fed; I can remember when mother was weaning her, feeding her with a spoonful of 'pobs' (bread and milk) and Virol. When mother died in 1929, Edna was taken up to Grandma Brunt at

Horton School. Mr Leech, headmaster.

Royal Cottage. We were taken to Aunty Marys at Brook House. The last time I saw mother, Mrs Walter Heath and Aunt Annie were with her and giving her ice to suck. Dad came to tell us she was going into hospital and he was crying. She died in the operating theatre.

When the funeral was held we were sent to Uncle Will's Poets Cottage. I seem to remember a stone sink with a rotary pump; the water came from a well outside. We read some religious newspaper. Later back at Fern Cottage, Sam said mother had gone to live in Heaven.

Ten days short of a year later in February 1930 dad was killed.he had been to Buxton for a load of lime and called to see Edna at Royal Cottage. Coming down Upperhulme bank, the fly wheel broke, a piece flew off and struck him on the head and killed him. Walter Heath had to take control and pull the wagon to a halt, saving further disaster.

At Royal Cottage. Norah, Sam, Mary, Edna and Joan Brunt.

We were at Yew Tree Villa, now called The Homestead. I went home from school to light the fire and we had normally fed when dad came home, often cheese and onions. This evening he was late so I went up to the Heaths at Smithy Cottage. Mr Heath was at home and they said Aunty Mary and Uncle Jack would be coming. We were taken to Brook House and told next morning that dad had died. Grandfather and Aunty Alice came up from Monmouthshire for the funeral. When it was all over they took me back in a small hired lorry with some of our furniture and belongings.

I still remember Saturday evenings when we sang with dad 'Farmers Boy' and 'Clementine'. There were no songs after mother died. Other memories are of rides in the steam wagon with bundles of silk waste for cleaning.

Horton School.

Roy Sant

My Grandad, Joseph Sant came to Trees Farm, Dunwood in 1916 from Hare House at Bradnop. It was a rented farm on the Dunwood Lodge Estate owned by Mr Thomas Hulme. Dad left the Trees in 1927 and came here to Dunwood Lodge which he bought from his uncle, who owned it by then. It was the year Stanley Pool burst and he had to fetch the cows up from down the field on the horse's back, the cows actually swam across the brook, it was that bad. For two days it had never stopped raining.

Roy.

John Brown on load, Grandad Sant, Felix Stubbs, Grandad Stubbs, Derek Jones and Bob Stubbs.

I was born here, in the front room. I went to Longsdon School and then Endon and then started work at home on the farm. In 1968 I started working at Newcastle Market as a drover for Heywoods Auctioneers. I was paid £2 a day; by the time the market closed, it cost £2 to park your car! Then I started at Leek market as well and continue to do so.

At home we always milked cows. We had electric in 1936 and dad had a milking machine the same year. It was an Alfa Laval supplied by John West and costing £100. We bottled and sold milk locally until 1957 when we sold the cattle and bought in TB Attested cattle and afterwards just sold the milk to the Milk Marketing Board. Our milk went to Manchester to Lancashire Hygienic Dairies. Wilf Allen picked the milk churns up for Moss and Lovatts. He worked seven days a week, rarely having a day off for 23 years. I think there were 17 pickups on that round. We had a bulk milk tank in 1972 and continued to sell milk until 2004. There are very few of those dairy farms left now.

In 1950 we bought a new Fergy T20 petrol tractor costing £335. Three gallons of petrol would last us a week. In 1960 we changed it for a Massey Ferguson 35 with a Bamford B48 pickup baler for £700. We kept that baler for 17 years and had a new one costing £1950 and they allowed me £700 on the old one. We've still got the tractor. We've always made hay for the cattle; very rarely silage except in '57 when it was very wet and we never finished mowing that year - the same as last year, 2008. The only 2 years all the while I've been farming when we've not finished the hay.

When the Fernyhoughs came to Stanlow in 1953 they walked their cattle from Yew Tree Farm at Basford over Park Lane which was closed while they came over. Dennis baled for us until we got our own baler. He did baling for a lot of people and really enjoyed it. He was always very particular about his work and kept his machinery immaculate. We helped him with his cattle, bought cattle from him and supplied store cattle to him when he went out of milk. He was the last person in the area to grow and combine corn.

Dad went over to our neighbour Mr Wilson at Taylors Green one day. He was digging in a ditch. Dad said, *'What are you digging for?'* He replied, *'Bull had me down and I lost me teeth!'*

Anthony West, Bob and Felix Stubbs, Honeysuckle Lane.

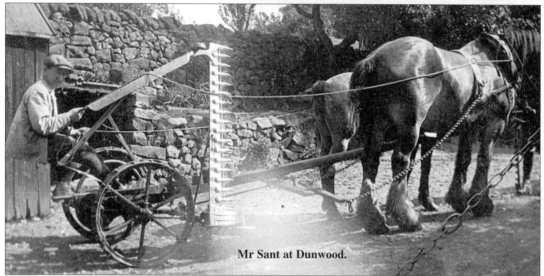

Mr Sant at Dunwood.

Sant family at Dunwood Lodge, late 1940s.

Great Grandad Sant and son Jack.

Bob and Felix Stubbs with
their first baler, 1956.

Below L to R:
1. Felix Stubbs snow ridding
Dunwood Lane.
2. Dad - William Sant - in
front of Dunwood Hall with
Aunty Nellie.
3. L to R: John Brown, Tom
Davenport, Jim Malkin.
1930s.

Felix and Bob Stubbs at Trees Farm

At Lower Dales, Dunwood Lane.

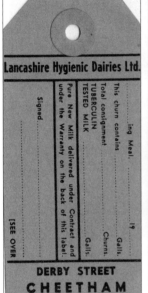

Lancashire Hygienic Dairies Ltd.

This churn contains ..... ing Meal.

Total consignment ..... Galls.

TUBERCULIN TESTED MILK

Pure New Milk delivered under Contract and under the Warranty on the back of this label

Signed ....

19 ...

Churns .....

Galls.

[SEE OVER

DERBY STREET

CHEETHAM

Warranted Pure New Milk, sweet, clean and marketable with all its cream and without the addition of any preservative.

Warranted also to be Tuberculin Tested Milk produced and sold in accordance with the statutory regulations which apply to such sales.

1. Sold by Signatory to Milk Marketing Board under their prescribed contract.

2. Sold by Milk Marketing Board to :— **LANCASHIRE HYGIENIC DAIRIES LTD.** under the Board's Sale Contract.

[SEE OVER

'Bobby' Bailey at Dunwood junction with A53.

Dennis Fernyhough and Joe Ogden harvesting at Stanlow.

Miss Gladys Fernyhough.   Mr Dennis Fernyhough.

Horton Church Bells (Ed. SH)

In Horton Church tower is a ring of six bells inscribed:

  No 1: Hark to our Melody
  No 2: Peace and Good Neighbourhood
  No 3: Prosperity to This Parish
  No 4: Abraham Redhall Cast Us All
  No 5: William Read, Richard Myatt, Churchwardens
  No 6: Unto This Church I Do Men Call
        And To the Grave I Summon All

The bells returning in 1979.

Courtesy Geoff Browne, Leek Post & Times

In 2003 a celebration was held for 'The 250th Anniversary of the Bringing of St Michael and All Angels' Bells from their Medieval Cistercian Abbey of Leek.' There has always been and continues to be an enthusiastic group of bell ringers. Walter Heath of Smithy Cottage, Gratton was a member for over 70 years and was Leading Bell Ringer for a lot of that time. Stan Gordon remembers in the early 1950s when he was a bell ringer that on New Year's Eve they started ringing for an hour at 8 o'clock and then supper was put on for them at the Crown. They then went back to church and rung the New Year in.

In 1979 all the bells were removed and taken to the bell foundry at Loughborough, completely overhauled and new headstocks added.

Current bell ringers are: Derek Sillito; Phillip Wood; Robert Barcroft; Eric Moss; Ben Dickenson; Roy Lovatt; Malcolm Cartlidge; Penny Lawton and Alice Wood.

HORTON

Joyce Sillito ATCL Sunday by Sunday

The pipe organ is known as the king of instruments, therefore I feel very privileged and honoured to be an organist. I attended Saint Michael's Church, Horton as a young child sitting in the congregation with my parents and brothers, later with my school friends in the choir and from my early teens as the organist. What qualifications do you need to take on this role you might ask? Perhaps a string of letters after your name; knowledge of the Church's liturgical year and the ability to improvise, to name just a few. However, a short time ago I read an advert for a church organist and the only requirement necessary was a good sense of humour. Perhaps a combination of all these would be the ideal.

To follow three separate lines of music and juggle with various organ stops whilst keeping an eye on what the vicar's up to at the altar must be very good exercise for the brain and to appear calm whatever the situation you find yourself in is something to strive for. Some time ago when I was preparing to unlock the organ console the key slipped from my fingers and fell underneath the pedal board. As a funeral was just about to take place, I wondered whatever shall I do? Confess to the vicar, panic or try to retrieve the key. Having thought the final solution was the best I proceeded to force my hand down between the narrow gaps of the pedals. What a relief when I found the key, but my fingers took some time to heal.

The playing of Anglican psalms was quite a challenge during my early years as an organist and I particularly remember the response from one of three old ladies sitting in the congregation, who was rather hard of hearing. After the play over of the chant she remarked to her friends in a very loud voice, *'I don't know that chant, do you?'*

When Winifred Beswick and I went to music lessons on a Saturday afternoon in Leek, we saw one of the three ladies at the bus stop. She was always jumping the queue; we couldn't resist joining in the game. You can guess who won.

These years spent at Horton Church have brought me into contact with many people who have shown me much kindness. I recall how Elsie Goodall went out of her way to walk home with me on dark winter evenings following evensong. Parishioners will often show a great deal of thoughtfulness and generosity. In particular I remember how pleasantly surprised Derek and I were to find that our wedding ceremony had been recorded by one of the church members. It goes without saying that the family has always been there to give me an honest opinion whenever it has been necessary.

I don't know whether Derek, my husband, has ever quite forgiven me for the time I locked him in the church tower. After a funeral had taken place I was the last person to leave the church, at least that is what I thought. I locked the vestry door before leaving. Then, accompanied by the Reverend Basil Peel, I walked to the Crown Inn for the funeral wake. Unfortunately, unknown to me, Derek had decided to carry out a job on the bells in the tower chamber. On discovering his predicament he climbed the spiral belfry steps to the top of the tower and on to the roof and shouted loudly. Basil Heath, who was busy filling in the grave at that time, heard a cry for help. I don't think, at first, he knew where the voice was coming from!

One of the pleasures of playing the Church organ is in sharing a small part of people's lives. Perhaps, with a young couple planning their wedding music when the bride excitedly tries to decide what music to come in to or go out to and the bridegroom nods in agreement at various intervals. There are also the sad occasions when I play for the funeral of someone very close. At these times, as of course for all services, the right choice of music is extremely important.

Alan Hudson

When we were kids, we lived at the Hollins, Horton. There were 5 smallholdings and they all used to send 2 or 3 churns of milk. Joe Hill from the top farm used to pick all the churns up with his horse and float and meet Bob Heathcote's milk lorry at the bottom of the Lea below the school. (Now the village hall)

One day Bob Heathcote met Major Greaves in his big car, who then lived at Horton Hall. Neither of them wanted to reverse but eventually Bob did. Then the end of one of the metal rails which held the milk churns on dropped off and dug in the road, which took the weight off the back wheels and so he could neither go backwards or forwards. We children had to go back to school to get a pick and shovel to dig a hole in the road to free the bar. I always remember that.

Dolly.

Dolly and Roger Barnacle at The Hollins, 1955.

Melanie Myatt

It would not be right for a memoir of Gratton to be published without a mention of probably its most famous son - George Heath, the Moorland Poet. He was born at Hall Gate (now sometimes referred to as the Poets Cottage) on the 9th March 1844. He died there on 5th May 1869 at the tender age of 25. I was first introduced to the work of George Heath by Alice Myatt one summer Sunday afternoon 20 years ago. I can remember an old book covered in brown paper lying on her knee open on page 180; the name of the poem Minnie, Edith and Lizzie. She explained that her Mother was the poet's niece and was the Minnie in the poem. That was enough to ignite my imagination and curiosity.

George Heath's own life is worthy of any tragic hero created by the great romantic novelists. A sensitive young man his short life witnessed the hard toil of living off the land, poverty, illness, the heartbreak of lost first love and the deaths of beloved sisters through childbirth and tuberculosis, the same cruel disease which later claimed his own life.

With the guidance and support of his friend Herbert Wilson Foster he strove to educate himself so that he might put down his own thoughts in words; together they shared a love of the countryside

Poet's Cottage, Gratton about 1970.

and nature around them and with the motto 'Steadily onwards' supported and encouraged each other to reach their goals. HW Foster achieved his artistic ambitions gaining a scholarship to study art in London and having work exhibited at the Royal Academy. His work can be seen on the first pages of the Memorial edition of George Heath's poems in the form of a portrait of the poet.

George Heath's poems and diaries depict just how hard life was for the land workers at that time and how death was all too frequent a visitor, but they also show how important family, friends, community and his deep Wesleyan faith were to him. To his Mother he wrote:

> Never shall I cease to love thee,
> Never, never once forget.'

His own fear of being forsaken and forgotten did not come to pass. It was those very subjects that filled his poetry which made sure his name was not forgotten - his family, friends and community. Together they worked to erect the magnificent headstone in Horton Churchyard which was designed by HW Foster and produced editions of his poetry so that today 140 years after his death he is still talked about, written about and even has his own website.

Ed. Next door to Poet's Cottage is Gratton Hall where the writer, poet and critic Thomas Ernest Hulme was born in 1883. He was killed on Flanders Field in 1917 and was one of the 'war poets'. There is a window dedicated to him in Endon church. His grandfather, Thomas Hulme built Dunwood Hall. SH

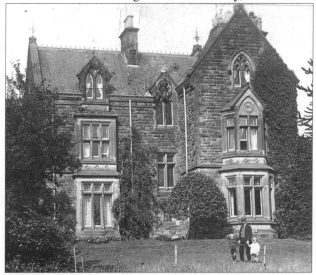

Dunwood Hall.

Nelly Snape

I was born at Henridding Farm in 1911; my grandparents, Jacob and Elizabeth Hall were there. They moved to Blackwood Grange from where I went to Horton School with my sisters Betty and Alice.

Henridding Farm.

We used to get up early and find and fetch the horse and cows in and help start milking before having breakfast and then walking to school. There was porridge for breakfast and bacon cooked in front of the fire. Sometimes cinders fell out of the fire and on to the bacon; my grandfather used to swear about it but they ate it just the same.

In holiday time we went to Leek by horse and trap with granny and grandad on the front and us kids on the back

Aunt Emmy Hall.

frightened to death of falling off. We had no money to spend but I remember we had a cup of tea somewhere.

Dad gave me the money for the rent and I had to go down to Heaton's offices in Endon once a month to pay it.

I left school at 13 and went to live in with the Heaths at the Ashes, where again I helped to fetch the cows and tie them up in the shed, help to milk, get the horse to the float and help to throw the big churns on ready for the rush to Rudyard station for 8 o'clock. I had to help get the children off to school; I was big Nelly, and there was little Nelly.

On the backyard was a copper boiler built into the breasting wall and it had a metal lid on. The washing was done out there. Alec Heath was staying and he was dancing on the lid with his clogs on, rattling away and the lid worked to one side and his legs went in and Johnny had to hold him up till someone came and lifted him out. He scalded his legs.

I had no money, just my keep. I stayed a few years then I got a job with Mr and Mrs Makepiece at Endon. I was lucky; no more rough work. I was the housekeeper, I did everything for them. He worked in Stoke-on-Trent City Council. I worked for them for 21 years then Mr Taylor married their daughter and I worked for them until they died, then I stayed on in the house.

Uncles Bill & Joe Hall - the 'Little Men' at Blackwood Grange c 1920. They later moved to Butterton.

Courtesy Bob and Glenys Hall.

Reg Hill

My maternal grandfather Owen was a blacksmith down in Shropshire and he got kicked in the chest by a horse and died from his injuries. The family must have lived in a grace and favour property because as soon as he was gone, grandmother and the four children had to move and they ended up at Lyme House cottage on Devils Lane. It was rumoured that John Knight had some connection and it was his property that they came to.

Mother went to work in the laundry at Leek, walking through the fields to Bridge End and Leek and she later worked at the Maypole, a general grocery store. When she got back home, she tented the cows on the roadsides which is what people did then on smallholdings and she had to fetch water from the well down the fields at Lyme House.

Grandad Robert Hill was a veterinary surgeon on Leonard Street in Leek. He went round the farms on horseback and was a very good horse vet. He looked after Sir Arthur Nicholson's stud at Highfield. One or two queried the fact that he was a genuine vet but we have a bottle with his name on R. Hill, Veterinary Surgeon, MRCVS. He also bred horses and had one called Paxton which won a prize at the Greater London horse show in 1888.

Joe Embrey at Rowley Gate.

I was born at Blake Meadows, Horton then we moved to Gibraltar Farm, we rented it from Bill Heath at Great Longsdon and helped out with jobs like thistle mowing in lieu of rent. Dad had to cart drinking water from the well at Rowley Gate for us - two buckets full. The Embreys there were fond of shooting and I can see Joe now pedalling up Devils Lane with a couple of rabbits over the crossbar going to the Waterworks to swap for some beer.

I used to play with the Shufflebotham lads; we went fishing and tree climbing, all the things boys do. We used to go to Lomas's at Lapwing and Mr Lomas let us smoke a clay pipe, we were 9 or 10. We smoked bran, tea leaves, dog ends; they might have been choking us but it didn't matter, we suffered all that. I dare say I started smoking Woodbines when I was 4; dad used to sit me on his knee and say, *'Have a puff puff.'* He smoked 40 a day.

Bill Green and Jack Embrey.

Rowley Gate.

BELOW
Hill children near
Rudyard Lake late
1950s.

At the end of the war, to celebrate, I remember a torchlight procession in the village. I think we started from the Walkers on the crossroads and went down Sutherland Road, up Micklea to the New Inn and ending up at Stanlow where there was a big fire and Jack West let off railway detonators instead of fireworks. People carried a burning tin can on the end of a stick; it was quite a spectacle.

We moved to Bradshaw when I was 13 and there started the adventure of living next door to James Heath and his ventures. He was a great neighbour and we often helped him out. We've helped load turkeys all night - 3 or 4 wagons - with crates on from Craven Arms or Thornhills from Derbyshire.

Celebrations after the War.

Bradshaw.

Then one bonfire night there was a fire, thought to have been caused by a stray firework. I was bedding cattle down at about 8 o'clock at night when I saw these flames going up. The fire brigade came and evacuated us, the children were all wrapped in blankets. There were a lot of battery hens then and we were trying to release as many as we could. I can see my wife Barbara now running out of the top loft with a fire hose in her arms - a fireman in front and two behind and rats running everywhere. Some hens were lost.

Rats used to burrow in the deep litter beds of the turkey sheds and when the sheds became empty it was quite entertaining to have a ratting party. So on a Sunday morning about 20 of us would gather with terriers, block all the holes up and go in with sticks. You could easily get 100 a time. Of course nowadays professional pest control is a requirement of their farm insurance.

There is quite a bit of history to Bradshaw; it was a 17C coaching inn and allegedly Dick Turpin rode through. The brewhouse was above the road, where Harry Gritton used to live. There were fire shields on the front of the house. If you had a fire and the firemen came and you hadn't paid your money and got your fire shields up, they let it burn, it was a sort of insurance.

The fire shields.

John W Heath

I was born at Bradshaw Farm in August 1948. My dad, James would have a go at things, he liked a challenge; sometimes things worked and sometimes they didn't. He didn't mess about; he jumped in with both feet.

When I was at school we were milking cows, then in 1955 he decided to try hens in cages and ended up with 6,000. When I came home from school, he would often say, *'You'll have to get some eggs collected'* because with 6,000 hens in cages you had to go round several times a day collecting the eggs and filling buckets. We had dozens of galvanised buckets full of eggs, then they all had to be checked for cleanliness and cleaned if necessary before being packed into boxes. I remember I once wanted to go conkering and Dad said I could only go if I filled 10 buckets of eggs first, so I went into the corn bin and half filled the buckets with corn and put eggs on top. I had a real rollocking when I got back

Mum and Dad would often spend evenings and Sundays wiping and packing eggs. There was a lot of work to it, even though at that time battery hens were supposed to be the modern development.

We tried the first turkeys; 1,000 in 1959, then 5,000 in 1960 building up to 30,000 in 1966. The dairy cows and the hens went in the early sixties. We used to buy day old turkeys and rear them before sending them to JP Woods at Craven Arms for killing, processing and freezing. The lorries came regularly at 2am and we loaded until 5 am. Poults came every week and turkeys went out every week. I remember some went to Sun Valley Poultry at Hereford and we drew 2/6d a pound liveweight. We could be working for a shilling a bird profit when we supplied birds for processing. You were forced into a numbers game.

We started to sell to Thornhills at Great Longstone who paid 75% of what they thought they'd be worth on collection and the remainder when they had been sold. In 1966, Dad was expecting the remainder to be £6,000, a lot of money back then, but there was nothing because the trade was bad. We only killed a few ourselves for the Christmas trade; there was no other trade then.

1966 was a bad year for us all as my mother passed away. We also lost a lot of money through a disease known as Turkey X disease - it was something that came and went - perhaps in the breeding.

We also used to make and repair poultry crates, a fill-in job for the men. We had the timber cut to size in Portugal, eventually delivered by canal barge to Cheddleton and to the farm by truck. We used to assemble the wood in frames and build the crate up. We also mended crates for Thornhills, I remember the yard was always stacked high with them.

It was in the 1970s we started selling to local butchers, pubs and caterers. We started off with bronze turkeys and then white turkeys were introduced which were easier to pluck. It has gone full circle as the bronze have now made a bit of a comeback and we currently do a few thousand a year since fashion has changed. There were no regulations at all in place when we first set up; everyone just did

John and Jim Heath.

The plucking shed 1960s.

it the same way. We used to dry pluck and hang the turkeys, which is known as traditional farm-fresh turkeys. Then in the 70s the first regulation came and Environmental Health started to visit the farm. We became a licensed slaughterhouse in 1980 and began selling to wholesale markets in Manchester. This was a good thing as we had more trade throughout the year. This market peaked in the mid

plucking shed 1970s.

1990s and has now dropped right back, probably due to supermarkets. Most regulations have improved the job but one of the worst things to contend with is the foreign vets who are difficult to understand and each one seems to interpret the rules differently - some are obsessed with seemingly petty things.

Things have changed a lot since we started. Back in the 1960s birds were caponized with a hormone pellet injected under the neck skin. This made the stag birds put on more fat and easier to sell. There was also in-feed medication routinely but legislation has changed all that and now virtually all medication is banned.

At Christmas you could make a good profit but the rest of the time was just to stay in business. It has always been a very sociable job with plenty of customers and staff coming and going. I enjoy the buzz and challenge and wouldn't have wanted to do anything else.

Rex Heath at Bradshaw.

Victor Moss loading muck at Little Bradshaw.

Courtesy John and Anita Moss.

Victor Moss's milk being picked up by Moss and Lovatt's at Little Bradshaw.

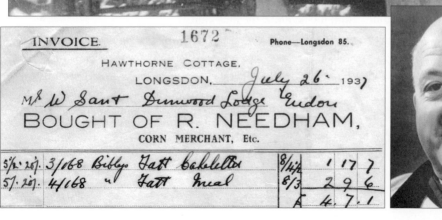

INVOICE.   1672   Phone—Longsdon 85.

HAWTHORNE COTTAGE,

LONGSDON, *July 26* 193*7*

M* *W Sant Dunwood Lodge Eudou*

BOUGHT OF R. NEEDHAM,

CORN MERCHANT, Etc.

5/2·20.	3/168	*Biblys Fatt Cakelles*	8/4½		1	17	7
5/·20.	4/168	*u Fatt Meal*	8/3		2	9	6
				£	4	7	1

Revd. Herbert Barton.

Eric Needham

In 1931, dad, Robert Needham, bought Hawthorn Cottage at Longsdon. He was always known as Bob and was then employed by Biddulph and District Agricultural Society as a salesman in the Leek area. He started his own business in 1936 operating from local railway stations and using Moss and Lovatt of Rushton and H Whittaker of Macclesfield and other local hauliers, collecting animal feeds from Manchester and Liverpool and delivering to farms.

Mr and Mrs Robert Needham
and grandson Martyn.

In the summer of 1939 a warehouse was built at Longsdon by Jack Findlow of Meerbrook and in late August he purchased a brand new Bedford truck enabling him to do his own local deliveries. However on the last Sunday in August, two men from the Ministry of Defence arrived and after a long 'discussion' - I could hear them arguing - they commandeered the vehicle and our driver had to deliver it to the army at Aldershot. War was declared a few days afterwards.

This started a very difficult time for dad; two days before war started, his driver, a reservist was called up and all the way to mid 1944 all the other drivers were called into the services. Three of them came back to us after the war finished. One man came to work whenever he was on leave; one morning he knocked on the house door and asked dad to be his best man.

So with the shortage of drivers it was a very hard time; dad delivered animal feeds in the daytime and office work was done at night. So they were 17-18 hour days, it was just a good job the telephone wasn't as busy as in later years.

One morning there was a knock on the front door. A black American was asking for a drink of water; he was walking from Hanley to Blackshaw Moor having missed the Liberty Truck provided.

Animal foods were on ration controlled by coupons from the Ministry of Agriculture to the farmers who traded them for food from corn merchants of their choice. In 1953 rationing finished, a blessing in some ways because of the paperwork but for a while it was chaotic because you didn't know where you were; it was like a free for all.

Dad joined the Home Guard which was based in Longsdon Memorial Hall for training and weapon usage and cleaning. On one occasion, someone's rifle went off; the bullet ricocheted into the end wall, along the ceiling, off the other end wall and through the piano, so luckily only the piano got shot! Dad was driver to the area CO taking him around the other Home Guard stations. It was all night driving in the blackout - good job he knew the area well.

In 1948 the office was moved from our front room into an office in the corner of the warehouse. Various sheds and garages were constructed again by Jack Findlow. In 1953 the firm was registered as Robert Needham and Sons Ltd. In August 1963, dad died aged 60 and the business passed to myself and my brother Harold. It had operated for 60 years when in 1996 we merged with a company from Uttoxeter.

In 1945, dad became a member of the Memorial Hall committee serving until 1960 and was also a member of Longsdon Parish council for a similar number of years.

One amusing incident I remember was when the vicar, Reverend Barton was trying to lose weight; he was rather large. So he used to come over the road to the warehouse to use the firm's weighing machine to check his weight and see if he'd made any progress. It amused us to see him step onto the scales, taking off his hat but keeping it in his hand while we weighed him.

Charles Heath

There have been Heaths in the Horton area for generations. I never knew my grandfather Abel, but dad told us that he was farming at Blackwood and lost his cattle with a disease, possibly Rinderpest, which caused him to become a stone mason but he also turned to drink. I believe he was a very good stone mason; he was one of the men who built the spire on Longsdon Church. He was once asked to build a fireplace for a woman at Brown Edge but could only go on a Sunday. So while he was doing the job, she sat with him and played hymns on a mouth organ to make it alright. In the first war he went building for Brunner Mond, who later became ICI, for the war effort. Uncle Harry went to fetch him home because he was poorly and said all he'd got to drink from was a tin can. He had silent pneumonia and died.

Abel.

Longsdon Church, St Chad's.

When mother and dad got married, they went to live at the Hollins, a smallholding at Horton. I remember mother saying that her and dad once walked to Leek from there with sixpence between them to walk back with a few groceries and they were frightened to meet anyone they owed money to.

Dad went working at the Black Bull pit at Biddulph as a stoker or fireman. They used to have half ton wheelbarrows which were very finely balanced and they had to keep the carriageway swept clear for them, so one trick that was done was to put bits of slack here and there and when someone was coming wheeling their barrow, it might cause the barrow to tip over and they'd have to shovel it all up again.

He told us that while he was there, a chap was murdered - thrown down the pit. There came

NOTE: Rinderpest was a devastating disease of cattle. In 1865 an outbreak killed an estimated 400,000 animals and was the reason that the British government set up the first national veterinary service. Poet Heath would have witnessed this dreadful plague. Only now is it hoped that it has been successfully eradicated from its last refuge in Somalia. (S.H.)

a detective from Scotland Yard and he worked there for nine months as a miner, no-one knew and he got in with this fellow; he'd an idea who it was and worked with him, shovelling and he got that friendly until he wheedled out of him, *'He wanted killing, I'm glad I did it.'* Then the detective put his spade down and said, *'You're under arrest, you'd better come with me!'*

There were four pits close together and they had a team who were paid a bit extra and were expected to be able to be called upon to go down the mines and do rescue work in the event of a disaster. Anybody that signed on for it, then didn't go when called, had the sack straight away. Dad was on that team for a while. Sometimes he had to stay on for three shifts because the others hadn't turned up to take him out. Then the tuck shop would be closed before he could get any food so he had to borrow a sandwich off other workers to tide him over. And mother was at home doing the milking and looking after the kids.

There was Pointon's Wheelwrights and Joiners down Biddulph. Dad ordered a wheel barrow and ladder off them, a wooden barrow with an iron hooped wheel and when he called for them, Dolly Pointon, the daughter hooped the wheel while he waited and they'd made a long wooden ladder, so he put the ladder on top of the barrow and his bike on top of that and wheeled it from Biddulph over the top of Lask Edge and down into Horton when he came off his shift at the Black Bull.

They moved to Dams Lane Farm and then up to the Ashes above, where I was born. They took the milk to Rudyard station; dad told us it was always a rush for people to get the milk there to catch the train, horses could be galloping, some were only half broken in; just so long as they could go faster. One could be going up the bank to the station and one coming down and if the wheels hooked together, churns might slip out, lids come off and the milk be spilt. My father-in-law, Wilmot Turnock, used to take milk there from Gunside and he once told me that as he took the milk in a storm one day, lightening struck and seemed to dance upon the churn lids.

Bill Stonier worked at the Ashes and he once fetched a mowing machine wheel from Wests in Leek and took it to the Black Horse at Endon on the bus and then carried it up to the Ashes. He had a big raw patch on his back; it was cast iron weighing the best part of two hundredweight. He was only 15 or 16 and it was just so he could put it on and go mowing the same night. He was a bit mad; once when it was foggy, they couldn't find the horse so he took the shafts of the float and said, *'I'll be the horse'* to take the churns down the lane to meet the wagon. Dad was behind holding it back; it was alright for a little while, then he pretended to trot and it started to go faster and go out of control. He swerved from one verge to the other to try and slow down, dad couldn't hold on and he was lucky not to have tipped it over and been run down and injured. Dad gave him a good cossin.

We moved to Bradshaw where Mavis and Eric were born; there were now twelve of us children. A chap named Jim Ratcliffe lived next door and he'd got a nice young horse and Jack Brown who lived at Little Bradshaw had got a very nice float, all painted up and lined. So they decided to put the two together and go for a ride round Leek, Jim, Jack and me dad, to show this horse and float off. I think it was Jubilee day and there were flags flying and bunting everywhere and at the top of Mill Street something frightened the horse and it bolted, went round the corner, tipped the trap over; the horse was in Mill Street, dad was on Clerks Bank under the float, hanging on to the reins with a broken leg. He never went to the doctors; all he did was use a broom upside down for a crutch and kept going like that. He said he could always tell when it was going to rain after that, his leg would ache two days before the weather changed.

I was about four and was on a swing, it wasn't going hard enough so Dick got on with me,

An attractive RESIDENTIAL & SPORTING PROPERTY

KNOWN AS

GREAT LONGSDON FARM

£[...]

occupying an exceptionally pleasant and convenient position 5 minutes from the Main Bus Route, Leek to Hanley and Burslem and within two miles of Leek, comprising an area of

229a. 0r. 19p.

or thereabouts of Meadow, Pasture, Arable and Woodland with EXCELLENT HOMESTEAD and WATER SUPPLY as now occupied by the Vendors, the Executors of the late Mr. John Knight, who will give VACANT POSSESSION AT LADY DAY NEXT, (or earlier by arrangement) and not make any charge for Tenant-right.

THE EXCELLENT MODERN HOUSE

with Gardens and Orchard, occupies an elevated sheltered position and commands extensive and picturesque views. The accommodation comprises: Entrance Hall, 2 Reception Rooms, Houseplace, Kitchen, Larder, Dairy, 5 Bedrooms, Store Room, Tank Room and 3 Servants' Bedrooms. H & C Water Supply. Milk-cooling House.

The SUBSTANTIAL RANGE of FARM BUILDINGS conveniently arranged around paved yard, comprise: Shippons tying 64 Cattle with Fodderbins and Lofting over, two Stables for 5 Horses and Box with Lofting over, 2 Calf Houses, Bull House, Loose Box with Loft over, Barn, Tool House with Loft over, Corn Store, Mixing House and Grain Pit, Garage, 3 Cart and Implement Sheds and 2 Piggeries, also 4-bay brick and tiled Hay Barn having one bay converted into 6-stall Stirk Shippon with wooden lean-to Implement Shed at rear. Manure Yard. Water Troughs supplied from Ram. The Out-barns comprise 3 Loose Boxes in Nos. 5, 27 and 33, also wooden Implement Shed in No. 12.

The Farm adjoins the River Churnet, which affords an excellent supply for Stock. The Water Supply at Homestead is by Ram from Spring on the Farm.

The whole of the Valuable Timber, comprising matured Oak, Ash, Larch, etc., is included in the sale. The Shooting & Fishing Rights are in hand.

The Staffordshire County Council pay £10 per annum for the right to take water from Springs in Enclosure No. 23. The L.M.S. Railway pay £[?] per annum in respect of Canal Feeder.

The Vendors are not making any claims in respect of the unexhausted value of feeding stuffs consumed or lime applied, and it is a well-known fact that the farm has been intensively cultivated by the late Mr. John Knight during his occupation as Tenant and latterly as Owner-occupier for 16 years, following a family tenancy aggregating almost 400 years.

By instructions of the Executors of John Knight, deceased.

LONGSDON, near LEEK, Staffordshire.

LEEK 2 MILES.   HANLEY 7 MILES.

VACANT POSSESSION AT LADY DAY NEXT.

An attractive Freehold and Tithe Free

Residential and Sporting Estate

known as Great Longsdon Farm, and Gibraltar Farm.

For sale by Auction by

J. OAKES ASH & SON

at THE SWAN HOTEL, LEEK, on Wednesday, 29th January, 1936, at 3 o'clock prompt, subject to conditions.

To view and for further information and to inspect plan apply on the premises or to the undermentioned:

Auctioneers: Solicitors:

J. Oakes Ash & Son, Leek.   Messrs. Bishtons, Leek.

the swing broke and he fell on me and broke my leg. They carried me to the house and left me on a pig bench by the door for mother to find me. Dick went off to work at Lyme house and Vera went off too. Joyce had to get up early and go down to the Tanyard at Endon and get Dr Swann to come before she went off to school. He came and put some splints on.

Great Longsdon came up for sale and it was bought by Wood and Wain. Mr Wain was a solicitor from Macclesfield and Mr Wood a farmer, councillor and JP. They were friends and bought it as an investment paying £7550 for it and Gibraltar Farm. So they were looking for a tenant; Mr Wain went back to Mr Wood, *'I've got two likely ones; one has money but no family, the other has a large family but no money.' 'That's our man, someone who'll work to keep the family,'* replied Mr Wood - and that's how we got it.

I started Longsdon School from Bradshaw at Christmas and we moved up to Great Longsdon at Easter 1936. Tom and Dick had moved before us and grandad Docksey had gone to stay with them. He made porridge for breakfast, dinner and tea; they were fed up of it.

Before the war, we used to do timbering, splitting hedge-laying stakes which were sold for sixpence each and oak piles for wire fencing, 2/6, but they could last for 100 years. You laid the saw along the wood to measure where to cut it, 5 foot. Us kids had to help dad cart stuff home on little sledges when snow was on the ground. Rex, Ronnie and me had a home-made sledge each - old ladder sides and a tin lath off a bed underneath which you rubbed with a rusty file to smooth up.

There was a great big ash tree between us and next door that was cut down, it was a very hard winter, a lot of snow and we carted all that wood home. It was that cold, when you picked steel splitting wedges up, they stuck to your hand.

We used a 5 foot cross-cut saw, two on one end and one on the other. The older lads did the sawing and the rest of us had to pick the sticks and all the bits up and cart it off for firewood, we had to keep tidying up all the time. If we cut a tree down in the wood it all had to be carried up the steep parts till they could get to it with a horse and cart. A timber firm had been and bought a lot of trees and left a lot of branches which all had to be cleared up.

If there was a tree going a bit dead, we would cut that down but we weren't allowed to cut other trees down until it was our own place, just clean up. Harry Goodwin once bought a lot of larch for pit props at Whitfield Colliery. Different farmers bought the stakes. Any big timber went for pit props. Leo Ferns was killed loading timber down at the station. He was on a timber 'drug' which was being unloaded under the three legs when the chain broke and the tree fell on him.

We grew a lot of potatoes to sell around the village and to the Co-op shops in Leek. £6 a ton delivered in hundredweight Hessian sacks. We got that used to weighing potatoes; you could fill a bag and lift it - *'That's about a cwt'* - put them on the scales and you were one or two potatoes over or under. Dick and Tom used to take a horse and wagon load down to Leek and the horse used to come home on her own - they lay on the wagon counting the money as she came up Ladderedge.

We had to take bags to the village with our bikes; they'd riddle a bag through the crossbars and you'd get it there, riding downhill with legs astride and have to tip your bike on one side and lift it off the bag, then get it into their back kitchen or coal shed.

If there was snow on the ground, we took them on the sledge and a few turnips as well, we used to grow them and cabbage and carrots. When we'd finished, we had a run down the bank opposite the chapel with the other kids and sledges. My old sledge made out of an old ladder could always go faster and further than a fancy shop-bought one.

I once went playing with Jack and Norman Rogers for half an hour when we'd come out of school early one day and when I got home, I had my backside kicked for going playing instead of going home to do jobs.

Mother, Ethel Heath.

When we got home we had to get changed and get stuck in straight away; throw grains up out of the grain pit, pulp turnips and get some chop; there was always a ruck of chop cut. Then mix all this together, perhaps with potatoes to make lickin for the cows when they came in from the fields. Then milking by hand, go up the lofts putting hay down if necessary, then running round the fields shutting hens in. There were several cotes so each person would go in a different direction, then change over, do one run one week then change the next week.

Rex and me were left at home one day, the others had gone down the fields; I was about 7. Harry Williamson came with his little truck with some corn on and backed up to the barn door. He was on his own, so to save him getting on an off, we got on and pulled the sacks to the side of the wagon for him to lift off. When we'd finished, he was that pleased, he gave us 2 shillings

Johnie, Charles, Hazel & Betty Heath and Alan Wheeldon.

and took us to Shentons shop where we bought some sweets. When dad found out we got belted for spending the money.

Harry always came for the order the day before Reg Whittles came round. If we had off Whittles, a chap named Arthur Bennison used to come with two horses and a dray delivering the corn. They were big horses and could really step out. He used to deliver to local farms not too far out from the Leek mill. Whenever he used to put his foot on the steps to get on the wagon, the horses would start off with a lunge and he had to grab the reins and sit down quick. He had a thick bag over his legs and another over his shoulders to keep the weather out and we used to call him Blueface. We used to have a barrel of beer and a barrel of burdock for harvest time and keep it down the cellar and they used to say if you had some beer and then a drink of milk you'd be sick and Rex and I used to do that on a Sunday night to try and make ourselves sick so we didn't have to go to school next day. But it never worked.

When the barrels were getting empty after harvest, we put them outside on the milk dock with a mug and Arthur Bennison used to come and collect them with his horses, and bring some corn and he used to sit there and drink this flat ale; how he drank it, I don't know, then he'd go across the fields to Devils lane and go on the rest of his round.

When we were going to school, Ted Salt had a horse and cart which Gilbert Holdcroft, a small fellow drove. He went round collecting ashes and rubbish and took it to an old pond on City Lane to fill it up. Another day he'd go round with a night soil cart; like a tank with a lid on the top and collect that and then go on different farms and let it run out of the back as the horse walked along. I suppose the council would pay them.

We used to cut the corn with a mowing machine with reaping tackle on. There were two horses and two men riding on, one driving and the other using the reaping tackle; he was using a 'gate' to gather the corn on. He had a rake which he pulled the crop on with from above the knives, then when it was full - enough on - he dropped the gate and slid the crop off enough to make 4-6 sheaves at a time. Other people were posted around the field to tie them up and us kids used have to go round making bonts for them. You picked up12-14 pieces of straw, split them, put the heads together, give it a twist and turn it over then put it on the floor and put your foot on it, then they'd put their sheaf on it, twist it round and tuck it under and that was your sheaf made.

When we started to use a binder, we still had to mow around the field and tie all that up and mow any laid places out, so that none of it was wasted and when we were haymaking, all the corners and edges were hacked out with a scythe and thrown into the field and we had to go round and rake all the outside in so the horse rake could pick it up when it was hay ready to carry.

Our next door neighbour had a binder but his horses weren't very powerful so we used to take ours, three of them to do the corn cutting but he always rode on the binder and we had to do all the stooking, making the kivvers.

The binder was a big improvement, it made a nicer, more uniform sheaf, so it was easier to make a stack; it was less work, saving manpower and using twine instead of straw bonts, so it was easier to cut a piece of twine when it came to thrashing.

When you were feeding the thrashing box, you didn't just throw the whole sheaf in; some had a self-feed like a rake which only let so much in at once. You could tell if a lump had gone in, it could almost stall and it wouldn't be thrashed clean; grain would be left in the straw.

In the winter of 1947, we were thrashing up the road in the shed. When we started, a stoat came off the top of the shed. Old Taffy Belfield said, *'There'll be no rats in here.'* But when we'd got nearly to the bottom of the bay, it was moving, so Sam Hine stopped the box and we put some netting round, loosed the dogs and got some sticks and caught a big barrowful of rats. I've never seen so many. We didn't get them all then and after we'd finished, we left the barrow and stoats and weasels came fetching them. They were so hungry, we were always seeing them.

We came with three horses and ended up with 4 or 5 work horses and bred 3 foals a year which were later broken in, some we sold, some we kept. We once bought a horse from Bob Plant

The family. Ron, Dick, Johnie, Mavis, Tom, Charlie, Eric, Rex,
Joyce, Vera, Ethel (mother), Nelly, Ivy.

Harry Heath and family.

at Westwood; he was a bit naughty and had a crack in his front hoof. We had some 'chapanoint' ointment from Perkins to put in this crack every day. I'd done it one day, then Ronnie wouldn't let me do it, he'd got to do it. As he bent over the horse bit his backside.

The horses were taken to Perkins at Endon to be shod, we had to walk them there and back; I had to go when I was old enough. We'd one, a youngster and if you pulled on him to check him a bit hard, he'd rear straight up. He was big and black, a lovely horse. As we knocked off one dinner time, Dick chucked me on his back; he set off trotting up the cow lane and I daren't rein him in. As we got to the yard, I had to jump off, run by his side, talk to him and put my hand on his nose to slow him down; I was only a lad.

Old Isaac Hudson used to travel round with a stallion and Tom Bailey from Lask Edge. They had ribbons tied in their mane and tail and the tail was tied up.

We had our first tractor in 1938, a little International with a mower; both cost £280. It was bought up from Leek station on a little LMS Scammell artic and Jack West started it up and backed it off. Then we had a two furrow Lister Cockshutt plough the following spring.

Dick used to go ploughing for other people. When he was working at the end of Devils Lane for Bill Brown at Steele House, I carried him 5 gallons of paraffin from the farm all the way down Devils Lane when I got back from school, at least a mile away. Esso used to bring it and we used to tip it in 17 gallon churns.

If we were sowing grass seeds, we tried to do it before 9am when the wind often got up. In the first year the crop was known as seeds hay and in the second year it was known as 'bastard seeds'. We used a seed fiddle to sow them; dad always used a hopper though, sowing with both hands whether he was sowing grass seeds or corn. The grass seed was always undersown into the corn when it was about three inches high - either wheat or oats. Then when the crop was cut you should have a nice fresh grass and clover ley to follow. There were competitions and someone would come round to judge the quality of the ley.

In the middle of the farm is what's known as Welsh Clough, a very steep valley. There is a coal seam there and geologists would come chipping away at it. A friend of ours says it's the end of a seam which comes from Wildboarclough. Our water used to be pumped up from some wells there to supply the farm by hydraulic ram. If the clack had stayed down, you had to go down and hold the clack up till enough water had built up under it to hold it up. Then you couldn't start the ram for 12 hours until the wells had filled with enough water to keep the ram going. It used to take two thirds water to pump one third. Another well nearby used to supply Westwood School. There was a 2 inch water pipe from there down through the wood under the canal feeder and over the Churnet. There was a footbridge with a locked gate on it. Underneath were two RSJs and the pipe ran between them and up the other side of the valley. Phillips plumbers from Stockwell Street used to come and mend it occasionally. It was cut when the big water main went through to Tittesworth.

When that was put in, there were Irish men working on the job and one chap used to be on an old Nuffield tractor. We had some black Herefords with white faces and they were on the bottom ground under a big ash tree, all lying together in a circle. From up on the hillside, this Irishman had seen them and he thought they looked like nuns praying. He was very superstitious and wouldn't go any further; he said it was haunted and left the job. The story got into the Leek Post.

Down by the Churnet there, our neighbour found some wooden drainpipes that were put in by the monks from Dieulacress Abbey, but as soon as you take them out of the ground, they start to dry out and disintegrate.

Herbert Clews of Boot Hall on the reaper with four of his sons, 1925.

Threshing at
Great
Longsdon.
Peter Howlett,
John Heath,
Dick Heath,
and
John Johnson.

Making the sheaves - Albert, Fred and Arthur Clews.

Longsdon School c.1930.

Ron, Charles and Yo-Yo.

Charlie Smith, Longsdon Grange.

In the 1700s a Reverend Richard Jackson owned Great Longsdon and he gave it to Trinity College, Cambridge to endow the 'Jacksonian Professorship in Natural Philosophy'. The Knights were tenants for 400 years according to the sale catalogue in 1936. John Knight bought the farm from the college in 1919.

Uncle Harry, Uncle Jim and Aunt Hilda worked for him, living in until they got married. They told us lots of stories about his eccentricities. When he was going home from Leek; perhaps he'd had a drop of drink, Ladderedge then was only like a lane, the trees had grown over and a branch swept him off his horse. He was on the council so the next morning he had all the council men out and had all the trees lopped. He used to mount his horse from some steps by the stable; he'd go partway up and then drop onto the horse. It moved away one day and he fell head first and broke his neck. He had a silver plate put in his neck and when he rode after that, his head would bob forwards and backwards.

Uncle Harry lived at White Chimneys and Aunt Hilda lived at Rose Cottage on Devils Lane when they got married. When John Knight came back from Leek sometimes, feeling flush, he'd buy these smallholdings at £100 or so. He bought Westons Folly at the top of Ladderedge, Rose Cottage, White Chimneys; then if he got hard up, he'd sell one. He bought Rowley Gate Farm and took some fields to put to Great Longsdon before selling it again. Before he bought it, on the bottom ground is a big pipe which drains the land into the Churnet. He took Joe Embrey down there, who worked for him then, and made him find the drain, lift a pipe out and stuff a bag in it, so the ground wouldn't drain - and then he bought it.

Aunt Hilda.

We pulled a grate out with a big over-mantle and stuffed behind it were corn bills and bills for beer and whisky. Down the cellar there was a hole under the bay window which only us kids could get in - we got two cart loads of empty bottles out which they'd thrown in as they emptied them.

Three workmen slept up the back attics and used to store the empty corn sacks up there. One chap was cold because there was no tile bodging on, the wind would whistle through the tiles. Uncle Harry kept carrying these sacks and covering him up. He'd got them many over him, he couldn't get up the next morning, so they left him and JK had to shout for him.

At night, as soon as the grandfather clock started groaning to strike 9 o'clock, he'd get up to bolt the doors - if anyone was with him he'd say, 'Get off bed with you.' Uncle Harry and Aunt Hilda had been for a walk in the fields one night. They came back; Aunt Hilda went in while Uncle Harry spent a penny and he was bolted out. She had to creep down stairs later and let him in.

Near the end of City Lane is Keepers Cottage. There were once two big gate stumps and a huge gate which belonged to Great Longsdon. The man who lived in the cottage was the gate keeper.

Aunt Clara Hidderly lived at Little Longsdon. During the war she had two evacuees from Manchester to stay, Margaret Clark and Yolande Chette, who was Swiss. We knew them as Bonny and Yo Yo and played with them. Aunty Clara used to make frumenty at harvest time which was boiled wheat, thickened with a white sauce and nutmeg and cinnamon added. It was lovely, very filling but they didn't like it; when no-one was looking they'd take it to the sink and poke it down the drain.

Edgar Edge, George Wheeldon, Sam Hine, Arthur Corbishley, Joe Embrey, Charlie Harrison, ---* , Alan Hudson, ---*, Phillip Beswick, Harry Williamson (The Ashes), John Massey.

* Judges

At Harracles Hall c 1950.
---, Jack Hudson, ---, ---, Joe Embrey, ---,
Herbert Beech, Charlie Harrison.

**HEDGE-LAYING
COMPETITIONS
WERE POPULAR
IN THE AREA**

Harry Heath.

Jean Smith at Longsdon
Grange early 1950s.

BELOW
Reg Heath at
Summerhill Farm.

Photos courtesy of
Jean and Reg Heath.

Arthur, William and
Andrew Smith at
Longsdon Grange early
1960s.

Above: Jack Embrey and Sister Joan at Rowley Gate.

Left: Mary Billinge, Ethel Heath, Hilda Kennedy.

Below: Stanlow (Stonelowe) Hall.

Jack Bailey

We lived on a smallholding on Biddulph Moor called The Hollands. A neighbour of ours was Bill Pass and he'd got this load o' lime tipped up an' we got this 'andful o' lime - an' yer know 'ow they used t' put a bit in a tin an' a drop o' water on it t' blow the lid off. Well, we put it in the stable at 'ome. Bill Pass come down with Copper an' 'e sez ter me mother, *'Wheer's all this lime these lads'n pinched?'* Me mother sez, *'Wheer's this lime yer'n pinched?'* ter me an' our Bob. We opened this stable door an' when 'e sayd it; this copper sez, *'What the bloody 'ells up wi' thee Passy; 'ast they never put a bit o' lime in a bloody tin?'*

An' when yer went up through the first gate, 'e'd a great big ginger carthorse called Poppet an' we couldna get through this gate t' get t' school. So our Bob said, *'We will shift the bugger,'* and 'e got a piece out o'th' hawthorn 'edge an' gen 'im a jab in th' arse and it let go with both feet an' split the gate from top t' bottom! It's a good job we werena standin' close to it.

I remember when I wasn't very old, 'e bought the first President tractor and 'e said t' me mother, *'Can the lad come an' 'elp us t' cart some sheaves of corn.'* So I went an' I was standin' lookin' at this tractor an' 'e comes an' sez, *'Nah lad, whatever thee duz, never let me catch thee on that.'*

A footsill is where they walk in a mine t' get a certain stone for sharpenin' things; a whetstone; they got it from near Mow Cop. Instead o' goin' down a shaft, they used t' walk in; me brother did. Passy went workin' there an' Bob 'ad told the other blokes about the lime. They all sat round and said, *'Fancy Passy mitherin' over a 'andful o' lime.'*

With me friend, Norman Chaddock, we used go troutin' with us 'ands. We'd bin down near Rushton one day an' were that 'ungry walkin' 'ome, we got in this field an' got a turnip; we'd found an old tin can an' got the top off t' scrape it with. This bloke saw us; we set off runnin', gettin' away but then a chap on a motor bike come along an' picked 'im up. 'E caught up with us an' what a din, what a fuss over pinchin' a turnip.

We used get good trout an' people used say you'd get bitten by water rats but never in the memory o' man. We felt under tree roots in 'oles as black as a bag an' catch the biggest fish an' 'ad the water rats go past me fingers an' never touched us. One day, there was a big tree trunk, Norman was feelin' over one side an' I was th' other. This water rat jumped on the log an' sut i' th' middle. I said t' Norman, *'Luk at this rat 'ere.'* He said, *'What's up wi'thee Jack, we'n come fishin' not rattin'.'*

Jack Bailey.

Tom Bailey's place, top o' Biddulph Moor; we used go ridin' this donkey. It used go round the field then make for a 'ole i' th' edge an' pull yer off. Tom came out one day an' sez to 'is lad, *'Fetch 'im round Eric, I'll stop 'im comin' through.'* 'E stood th' other side th' edge with muck shovel an' whacked it one. It never pulled us off no more.

When I were schoolin', this night-soil cart came, they went round at night emptyin' toilets an'

Elliot Lancaster and his mum, of Whitefields. Mr & Mrs Lancaster used to keep the New Inn at Biddulph Moor.

came t' school in the daytime. Charlie Chaddock 'ad a big 'eavy 'orse an' they used sit on top o' the cart eatin' their snappin'-- cheese sandwiches. A big cart with big iron wheels an' two lids on top an' 2 or 3 bins 'angin' on the back. Norman 'ad go an' eowd th' orses 'ead when they went at night. It must 'ave been a helluva weight on; we could 'ear 'em comin' an' smell 'em quarter of a mile off at school. There might 'ave been 20 bins t' empty at Biddle Moor School. They emptied 'em on a field where we used 'ave go playin' football; yer could be kickin' paper up an' down. It was opposite Charlie Nags shop, they used call 'is missus 'split raisin'.

Owd Polly Lovatt 'ad a shop; when yer went in there were only just room go t' counter. On t' left was the paraffin with a pump on top an' yer put yer gallon tin under it, an' on the side was a great big round block o' cheese. On top o' that sut the bloody cat. No wonder it were good stuff. They never washed their 'ands after doin' the paraffin. She used say, *'I know why every body comes 'ere, I must sell the best bloody cheese on Biddle Moor!'*

Jim Nixon on Biddulph Moor; I went workin' for 'im an' 'e'd 'undreds an' 'undreds of 'ens. Later on 'e kept mink. They once went to a mink show at London an' I was left on me own. I'd the milkin' t' do, an' there was a very big incubator, 8-10 foot square which hatched 'undreds of eggs. First thing I 'at do before milkin' was turn a wheel, like a steerin' wheel which turned the eggs, an' then before I came 'ome at night I 'at turn 'em back.

I did all this; when 'e come back 'e sez, *'Righto, I'll look after th' eggs now.'* When I went in on Monday, 'e were that funny, I couldna mak out what I'd done wrong. His wife sez, *'As 'e said owt t' thee Jack?'* I said, *'No, why, what's up?'* *'He's turned all these eggs upside down.'* 'E'd done it before, overturned the wheel; it took from Monday till Wednesday t' clean the mess up of all the broken eggs. Normally after a week in the incubator, they used look through these eggs, candle 'em an' there came a bloke out of Potteries an' fetched the ones which weren't fertile an' they went for sponge cakes.

All round th' outside o' th' fields were these 'encotes. I 'ad go round with like a big muck barrer full o' corn. There were some I'd forgot fasten up an' the fox 'ad been; I've never seen so many dead 'ens. There was a big crop o' corn ready for cuttin' next door. I said to th' eldest brother, *'What do I do now?'* he said, *'Gather 'em up an' throw 'em amongst the corn, then when you go in the mornin', collect some 'ens out of th' other cotes an' put them in.'* That's what I did an' 'e never knew.

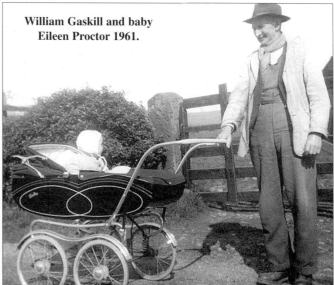

William Gaskill and baby Eileen Proctor 1961.

Ron Proctor with Graham and Una Brown.

BELOW
Billy and Arthur Deakin on Poppet 1950.

Photos courtesy of
Eileen Harvey.

BELOW
Elizabeth Jane Gaskill at
Shuttershaw with
Windsor and Bob 1951.

Haymaking at Moor Top c 1951.

LEFT:
William and Annie Proctor
with grand-daughter Jennifer.

**William Proctor
1950.**

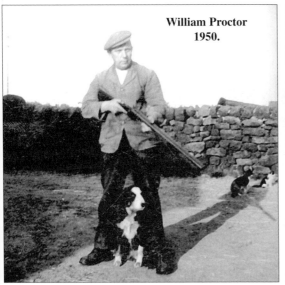

Ron Proctor 1966.

William Gaskill, Elizabeth Jane Gaskill with Graham Proctor, William Davenport* (centre), Mary Sims, George Sims.
* William Davenport emigrated to Canada before the First World War. He never saw his parents again and returned only once in 1951 when the flight cost was subsidised by the Festival of Britain. Photo taken at Dale House.

Ron and Graham, June 1950.

Winnie Hackney

My father bought Three Nooks Farm from my grandparents in 1945. I was three years old when we moved there; it was explained to me that he bought it to keep my stepbrother out of the war. I loved living there among the animals; we kept hens, chickens, turkeys, pigs, cattle and had a bit of arable - taters and turnips.

My father, Laurence John Brown was a likeable soul but firm about things. The cows were always milked at a set time. He was chairman of Horton parish council and chairman of Biddulph and District Agricultural Society for some years. He had to go to regular meetings over the shop on Derby Street in Leek and you didn't have to be late. Mum and I would go shopping in Redmans or Home and Colonial while he was in there.

My grandma, Agnes Brown had kept a little shop at Three Nooks selling general groceries. It was like a dairy while we were there with stillages round. We kept the eggs in there and washed and packed them into boxes ready for the Egg Board to pick up. When we had pigs

Grandma Brown at Three Nooks Farm.

killed the sides were put on the stillages and mum used to get that block salt and cover them in it.

Over on Biddulph Moor was Polly Lovatt's shop. There was a bell over the door which donged when you went in and this great can full of paraffin and in those days you didn't have bread wrapped up. It used to stink to high heaven of paraffin - you could have a bottle of paraffin then you'd ask for a loaf. Well, she'd been messing with the paraffin and go and pick the loaf off the counter or you'd ask for a quarter of toffee which were in those triangle bags - then she'd get her hand in the jar, she'd not wash them, still with this paraffin and Martha Ann Brown in the New Street shop was exactly the same. Everything stunk o' paraffin.

I've been told this story, another little old lady, Florrie kept another shop. If you went in there she might be by the counter or nowhere to be seen. Now you could see through the shop into the living end and she might shout, 'just a minute' - she'd be sitting on a bucket (you know) then come straight into the shop, they didn't bother washing their hands, and we're all still here aren't we. It felt like a Biddulph Moor thing, this paraffin.

Dad, Lawrence Brown, started this service on Biddulph Moor in the early 1930s, with Joe Turner and Dennis Sherratt.

Frank Proctor

In wartime I went to the War Ag office on Buxton Road in Leek to look for a job. They gave me one, tractor driving and ploughing. I'd done one week on an old TVO tractor worth nothing, so I went in on the Monday morning to see David Harvey. He said, *'How did you go on?'* I said, *'No use at all, I couldn't get on with that tackle; if I can't have a better machine, I'll finish.'* He said, *'You can have a crawler.'*

At Biddulph Moor. L-R: Enoch Proctor, -- Brocklehurst, Billy Birtles, Sheila Proctor, Derek Shawcross, Frank Proctor..

I never did owt else; it was ploughing every day in all weathers. You could get wet through; there were no cabs. Some of the ground was so sour up on the moors near the Mermaid, ploughing gorse and heather. I did a lot round Leek, Longnor and Warslow along with Frank Buxton and Jimmy Durose.

We lived on Biddulph Moor and afterwards I started collecting Hessian sacks from farms. I first started doing it a bit at nights and started trading with 'Botty' -

Harold Bott at Congleton. He cleaned them and vacuumed them inside and out. Some had to be mended, darned with a little machine because there'd often be rat and mouse holes. Them as had no writing on the inside could go for printing again, turned inside out. Then back to the corn mills in Liverpool. Botty bought the sacks off me. I travelled all over picking them up, between here and Bakewell and down to Stone. On the farms round Bakewell I was known as Little Staffordshire Mon.

According to where I went and what luck I had, I could mostly pick up a 1000 to 1200 a day. I've gone sometimes and picked 16 or 17 thousand up in a day, buying from corn warehouses. They all had to be counted and handled by hand. I got up one Wednesday morning and didn't go bed till Saturday night. I took the bags home, unloaded 'em and sorted 'em into different sorts; there could be 9 or 10 different ones; what we called plain 'uns which could be printed again, different sizes and weight of Hessian. Then there were double marked 'uns. Then I fastened 'em into 25s and had load 'em up again. Some I took straight to Liverpool, everyone paid different.

It was pretty fair o' work but it paid all right, according to how many you shift, like any business. I did it for about 20 years; when foot and mouth came in the late 60s, that about jiggered it.

At Greenwells Filling Station, Lask Edge. L-R: Enoch Proctor, Derek Shawcross, Frank Proctor.

Milking the goat,
and running a wood shavings business.

Mavis Dalton

One memory that stands out in my mind as a child at Great Longsdon was when the war was on and I was about nine years old. We had all the beds moved from upstairs down into the cellar for safety. I used to be terrified every time I heard the Jerries coming over and hear the sirens going. I'd feel sick and couldn't sleep.

Then one night when I did sleep, a bomb fell down the Ram Field as we call it and I never heard a thing. It made a big crater in the field and shrapnel sliced off pieces of the hedge and passed through the hencote in the field making holes in the sides but never touching the hens inside.

People came from all around to have a look and to take back bits of shrapnel as a memento.

Donald Heath

My grandfather was Henry Heath a wheelwright who lived at Tomfields, a twenty acre farm at Horton. Grandma was Elizabeth Heath from Birch Trees Farm and Morridge Side, Bradnop before that. So a Heath married a Heath. They kept about half a dozen cows and had a little milk round locally; it would be by churn and ladle then. They always supplied the Miners' Home and on a Saturday grandma would go on the train from Rudyard to Macclesfield where she had a stand there by the Town Hall where she sold cream.

They had six children, my father was Steven and as a family we lived at Stone House which used to be called Grindlestone Edge. Dad was gardening at Endon until the war when he took the farm over.

Grandparents Henry and Elizabeth at Tomfields.

Tomfields Farm.

Nancy Heath.

I can remember Charlie Harrison living at nearby Heath House. He was known as Charlie Dick and used to go round castrating shire colts and he was very good at it. Then he'd sell the 'sweetbreads' to the Rudyard Hotel to cook as a delicacy.

I can just remember the General Strike of 1929. It was a bad time; a lot of people were out of work and tramping the roads even. I left school in 1937, aged 14 when things were just beginning to get a bit better. I went to be an apprentice joiner but they wouldn't have you until you were 16 so I had to work with dad until I ended up at Critchlow's builders' yard by the old smithy at Endon.

My great uncle George was at Spite Hall at Rudyard; they had a thriving business there, they had big parties, boats on the lake and a coal business, but when the war came it faded away. I used to go down on a Saturday afternoon doing odd jobs there and when the war came, the bloke who worked there was George Birch and he was in the Home Guard and he said to me, *'Would you like to join up?'* This was October 1940, I was only 17 and signed the paper. When I got home and told dad, he went mad - he'd been in the First War and got gassed. Well, it was too late.

In 1941 I went to the Potteries for a medical for the Air Force but was deferred until I was 20 because I was an apprentice. When I went again, I dropped a clanger - they passed me A1 and then sent me next door where an Army Captain sat there behind the desk. I thought, *'I've had it now.'* He asked me a lot of daft questions as they do. So by then they'd transferred me to the army; I didn't get a chance to go in the air force.

I was called up into the Warwickshire Regiment and that was the end of that; I was an Infantryman - my dad wasn't very happy about that. After a few weeks I got posted up to Shrewsbury where I was supposed to be going into the Staffords there but it was the Kings Shropshire Light Infantry. I did 10 weeks there and was then posted to Richmond in Yorkshire. I left KSLI and went on a signaling course for three months learning Morse code and that. When I'd finished there it was back to Shrewsbury where they were getting a draft ready to go somewhere. This bloke says to me, *'How old are you?'* I said *'I'm twenty.'* *'Oh, I've got a chap of 19; we'll change you round, let the young one stay behind a bit.'*

So I was put on the list to go to Market Rasen in Lincolnshire. It was the 8th Battalion Worcestershire Regiment; the third lot I'd joined and I hadn't been out of the country. I went abroad from there, ended up in Naples and then onto the Anzio Beachhead in the thick of it. It was the worst; sometimes the only thing to do was lie in a hole and pray. There was a lot of shellfire and at night they'd come over and bomb us.

Then it was into the 2nd Battalion North Staffords and onto Rome and Florence where one half of the city was German and one half British. It wasn't very good; the civilian population was mixed up in it getting hurt. There were a lot of bridges there and the Germans blew them all up except a very famous old one, the Ponte Veccia. We had to build 'Bailey' bridges across the river.

This was in the summer of '44 and as autumn came on we moved up into the mountains onto the Gothic Line in the Appennines. We were up there most of the winter in the snow in fixed positions holding the line. My friend who was with me all through Italy got wounded sitting beside me. We were in a mountain hamlet in a building with no roof on it and six or seven of us living in the cellar. Then two of us would take turns to be on guard and man the machine gun. It was a Browning pointing through an opening like a pitch hole in a barn, level with the ground where it sloped away. It was an American gun that they'd left us.

So there we were on guard through the night; the Germans knew where we were, they were down in the valley and it was very bad with mortar fire. We could hear it going off and so count the number of rounds going over. This time, about 5am, we heard these 5 thumps, then it was about 20 seconds, the time of flight as they went up through the air. We heard 4 come down, we never heard the 5th - it was a great big blue flash, we never heard a sound and it dropped right in front of this hole where we were and wounded my pal. A piece of shrapnel went right through his arm and into his body and I never got a scratch. We were covered in muck; that was a close shave.

The Allies had got that far and couldn't get any further. The weather was bad and we were stuck for weeks. We'd go in normally for a fortnight then out for 5 days. Everything, food and stuff, had to come up on mules to keep us going. They wouldn't bring water, you had to find your own; they could only load mules with so much, they didn't bring water or bread. We had to have biscuits - hard tack. The poor old mules got knocked about; you could find your way to the front by the dead mules. They had Indian troops looking after the mules, known as Muleteers, Mule Companies.

We were a number of divisions working for the American 5th Army under General Mark Clark. When the snow got really bad, we were out in these slit trenches. Everything would freeze up, even the guns; you had to keep firing them to stop them freezing. If you were in the slit trenches, it was just holding the line. They had you out in them for 24 hours and then bring you in. There was a little farm where you were given a hot meal. Well, we'd been out this night, we went back to this house and upstairs they were getting the food ready. They'd got a burner, what they called a 'Benghazi burner' which worked off a can of petrol. There were two blokes supposed to be cooking and a few more having a warm. I can see it now - this petrol can was leaking round the cap and this bloke was trying to knock it round with a spanner, it was too hot to touch and it exploded and blew all the windows out, frames an' all and a hole in the roof. Some of the blokes finished up in hospital; it's a wonder no-one was killed. It went off like a bomb; I only felt the blast luckily and wasn't hurt. When it came light the next morning there were great cracks opened in the walls, it's a wonder the house was still standing. All the stuff was out in the snow, everything was ruined.

Eventually they pulled us out and sent us to Palestine doing internal security against terrorists; the Stern Gang, some were called. We were outside Damascus when it came on the radio that the Japanese War had finished. Jews were coming from everywhere out of Europe and we had to arrest them and put them in an internment camp. Nobody knew what they were, they had no papers. We had to spend the nights on the beach catching them.

I was a corporal in the Staffords at the end. Our company became a training company in the Middle East. I was in the mortar platoon - 3 inch mortars. I got a motor bike for 12 months and a short Sten gun; you weren't let out of camp without you were armed. I got posted back in '47. We'd done 3 years with only one leave. Some of our lot hadn't been home for 4 years.

Pamela Hewson

My father, Lawson Birch was a director at Clemesha Bros and Birch silk mill in New Street, Leek; where Blakemore and Chell are now. He proposed to my mother, Noreen on the road near to Longsdon Church and when the piece of land there came up for sale, they bought it and built Wyn Dene in 1931. I was born there in 1933 and my sister Denise followed in 1938.

It was a lovely family home; we had garden parties and a Rose Queen there. Once, there was an accident on the main road and because we had two entrances, the traffic came through the garden. Another time we woke up to find a car sitting on top of the summer house.

I was very friendly with Wendy Sigley from next door and we used to go off on bike rides or have games in the garden. There was a play house with trains in, which father enjoyed. We used to go up to Mill Pond on Devils Lane and catch minnows and sticklebacks with little nets and tadpoles in season; we would have jars and jars of tadpoles. Wendy's mother, Gert was a strong character; she was a councillor and very involved working for the village.

Arthur Bailey from Fenton Fields had a milk round in the village with a horse and float. Denise sometimes went with him and loved to stir the milk and help to ladle it out. We helped them at haymaking using pitchforks to put the hay up onto the cart and then children were allowed on top of the load.

Colonel Howson had a tennis court at Nether Stanlow which we used to play on regularly and hasn't been used since. Miss Haig lived down the cutting there and we used to go picking fruit. She used to say, *'Be sure and close the little gate to keep the rabbits out.'* But there was a huge hole under the gate which they could get through. She used to travel to Leek in a three-wheel invalid carriage.

Father was in the RAF and spent a lot of time away in India during the war. We had an Anderson shelter built into the rockery in the garden and my sister and I thought it was marvellous to have our siren suits on and go out there. We had bunk beds and made tea and soup

The opening of the Longsdon Memorial Hall. Arthur Bailey of Fenton Fields is at right end, middle row.

'Fool's Paradise' 1963. Ada Green, Doreen Kemper, Mike Smith, Margaret Owen, Alan Jeffrey.
Centre: Doris Jeffrey. Front: Pamela Hewson, Betty Whittles.

One of my Christmas Nativity plays.

on a stove. The war didn't mean much to us except that daddy was away and we could hear the planes going over to Manchester. You had to be as independent as you could be; we grew our own vegetables and had chickens which I was terrified of. I used to push my sister in with a huge bowl of mash and they would flutter onto the dish.

After the war, the parish council treated the village children to an outing. A coal barge was cleaned up to take us to Consall for a picnic and sports in a field there.

The Longsdon Amateur Dramatic Society was formed at the end of the war; my father produced and acted in 'Forced Landing' in 1946 and we were involved in the LADS for many years. There was a lovely dance held on New Years Eve and Old Father Time came in at midnight.

Mr and Mrs Joe Billinge.

Annually at the church was Operation Cobweb. The men would go in and dust down all the high parts and then the ladies would go in the next day and clean all the pews down with vinegar. Then a day or two later they all went and waxed and polished. The church looked and smelled wonderful and then they all had lunch in the church room. It was fun to see them all in their overalls with their buckets.

Joe Billinge was the verger, he was wonderful and everyone's right-hand man. On one occasion I was off to dancing class with the children and there had been an argument, a door was slammed and the keys locked in the house. It was foggy and we started walking to the phone box to ring father. I was grumbling, Joe saw us and said, *'Have you got a problem?'* I replied, *'Yes, I've got the keys shut in the house.'* He said, *'You'll be the first house I've never got into, I'll come and try.'* He came with an enormous bunch of keys and opened the door straight away.

Garden fete at Nether Stanlow, home of Colonel & Mrs Howson. July 1951. Lillian Ryder, Village Queen, Mrs Howson, Pam Birch, Rev H Barton, Suzanne Hancock, Col. Gilbert Howson.

I started my education with private tuition at Holdenby on Denford road; there were four of us. Then to Moorhill in Leek, home of the Nicholsons; then to primary school in a wooden hut at the Nicholson Institute before going away to school.

I started teaching elocution in 1953; it is now known as 'speech and drama'. The pupils came to our house although I once took over a teacher's practice in Biddulph. I had to go by bus to Holden Bridge and then get another bus to Biddulph.

There have been mature students; I once had a policeman, and a vicar once sent his curate to help him to present his sermons. He used to come with his sermon prepared and he went on to become an Archdeacon. Some students have gone on to RADA and one has become the leading speech therapist in Cheshire.

I would have 12 to 15 students a week at my peak and was still at home for our children. I used to produce a nativity play for several years with my pupils in the village hall. I still have a few pupils by request; I'm now often teaching pupils whose parents came to me. I get a great fascination - each child requires a different approach. I love it, it's very rewarding.

ABOVE:
Longsdon Young Wives,
and husbands, entertain.

LEFT:
Carolyn West on Topsy.
Angela West on Babycham.

Longsdon Young Wives/Mother's Union coffee morning, Stone Barn Farm 1990. Front:Sylvia Dale, Margaret Thurston. Back: Ann Addison, Dorothy Hansell. Middle: Moira Middleton, Carolyn Busfield. .

Longsdon Rose Queen, crowning of Carolyn West by Alice Peacock. Attendant Julia Finney.
Courtesy of Tony Busfield.

Interior of Longsdon church 1914.

Gratton Smithy.

Frank and Geoffrey Heath.

Just after the First
World War, the
Heaton family of
Clay Lake, Endon.
They managed
estates throughout
North Staffs.

Frank Heath

I was born at Smithy Cottage, Gratton in July 1917. Goodalls kept the smithy next door and before I started school, I spent a lot of time round there watching the horses being shod. It was always busy; any farm of any size had a horse or two, Gratton Hall had about 8. There were always people coming, it was a sort of meeting place where they caught up on gossip because you might have to wait a couple of hours. When we were going to Endon School, such as Myatts would take their horses down and say, *'Send the lads home with them.'* So when we got back from school we were given a leg up and rode them back. Of course they knew their way.

Old 'Annie Abel' (Heath) used to deliver all the babies round Gratton, there were no professional people then. The Clews from Boot Hall used to call on my mother to do it when old Annie gave over. I've heard it said that her husband, Abel, pointed Dilhorne Church tower on his own, getting himself up and down on a rope with pulleys. One of their sons, Bill borrowed my dad's suit to go to his mother's funeral; they had very little money.

When I left school at 14, I went to Wardle and Davenports Mill in Leek for 6 weeks - my job was 'straightening women's hose'. Then I sorted them into a dozen pairs and they went off for packing. But I left, I wanted an outside job.

So in the 1930s I was chauffeur and gardener for Captain Woolley at Dunwood House. He had lodged with an aunt of mine at Rudyard and because there was a large family of us, he came and asked if there was anyone spare for the job when he went to Dunwood House. He became a brigadier during the war and afterwards became senior partner at Edwin Heaton and Sons, the old established estate agents at Endon.

There was three quarters of an acre of gardens to tend and I drove an Alvis for them and afterwards progressed to Rolls Royce, Bentley, Lanchester and Daimler. I had to wear a uniform and take Mrs Woolley shopping. It was 'Yes Madam, No Madam,' open and hold the doors and put the rug round them if they wanted it. I enjoyed it; they were good to work for at the time. People were very careful with their money; it didn't cost much to keep a chauffeur. Until I was called up in 1940, I never earned more than 45 shillings a week.

I went into the North Staffords as an Infantryman. I was in Ireland on a training course when it came up on the notice board that they were forming a new Corps called REME. Before that the work was done by RAOC, the Ordinance Corps. They took me off that course and in less than a fortnight I was in Ashton-under-Lyne on a 13 week mechanics course. I served with REME as a Craftsman until I left the army in Feb 1946.

I worked all over the place in various workshops such as Aldershot. I remember at Command Workshops at Guildford at the time of the push in North Africa, all the engines in 300 trucks were changed in one night, they all had a new engine before going to Africa. Normally two of us could take an engine out and put another one in in 3 hours, then someone would come and test it out.

I met my wife, Elsie Durber, when we used to go helping out at Myatt Brothers at Gratton Hall. She was a maid there, helping with the milking, housework, anything. At that time, most farms of any size grew oats for the horses and turnips for cattle feed and we used to help with harvesting.

I think I should have been a Hine really. I understand that my grandfather who we knew as Neddy Hine, seemed to have got together pretty well with my grandma Heath and there were several children which took her name. Of course it wasn't spoken of in those days but I think she must have had a struggle rearing those children and having no husband and I suppose people would have looked down on her.

Denford Farm about 1970.

Eric Grindon late 1940s.

Below:
Eric Grindon and sister Phyllis, milking in wartime.

Eric Grindon

I was born at Denford Farm in 1933; there were eight of us; five lads and three girls. Our mother was Eva Hine, born at Basford Grange and our dad, Fred Grindon was working there. He always said that he walked there to start work for the first time on Christmas day aged 13.

I remember the narrowboats on the canal going past taking coal to Brittains' Paper Mill at Cheddleton or to Boltons Copper Works at Froghall. They fetched it from somewhere in the Potteries, 20 tons at a time. The regular boatees were Fred Firkins who lived at Lockhouse, Tomkinsons and Jimmy Johnson who lived across the canal from us. One day he'd go to the Potteries and load up with coal, then next day go down to Froghall and unload and then back home again. I sometimes went with them when they unloaded. When they got to Froghall they had to throw it out with shovels into a barrow on the towpath and barrow it off. Of course when the boat was loaded, it sat low in the water and they only had to throw the coal two or three feet, but as the load got lighter, the boat came up in the water and the sides were higher to throw over and they'd be lower down into the boat too as the coal was thrown off. There'd only be two of them to throw the twenty tons off; it was a full time job for them.

Dad used to chop hay and mix corn for the canal horses and the boatees used to drop some slack off for us when they picked it up. Johnson's had two little fields and Firkins had pieces of land on the sides of the canal which they used. Tomkinsons had a piebald pony and regularly we saw them going down with it and after an hour or so you'd see the pony running back on its own and Tomkinsons running after it trying to catch it; I don't know how it got loose. They hadn't got big horses, they wouldn't fit under the bridges and the boats didn't take a lot of pulling once they were started. In the summer they used to clean one of the boats off and take all the kids in the area down to Consall for a picnic. We looked forward to that, there wasn't much else different; there were then about 30 kids in the Denford area; 8 of us, 3 Handleys, 2 Dockseys, 6 Sadlers, 5 Johnsons, 4 Firkins and 2 Birks. By the time I was twenty, the boats had more or

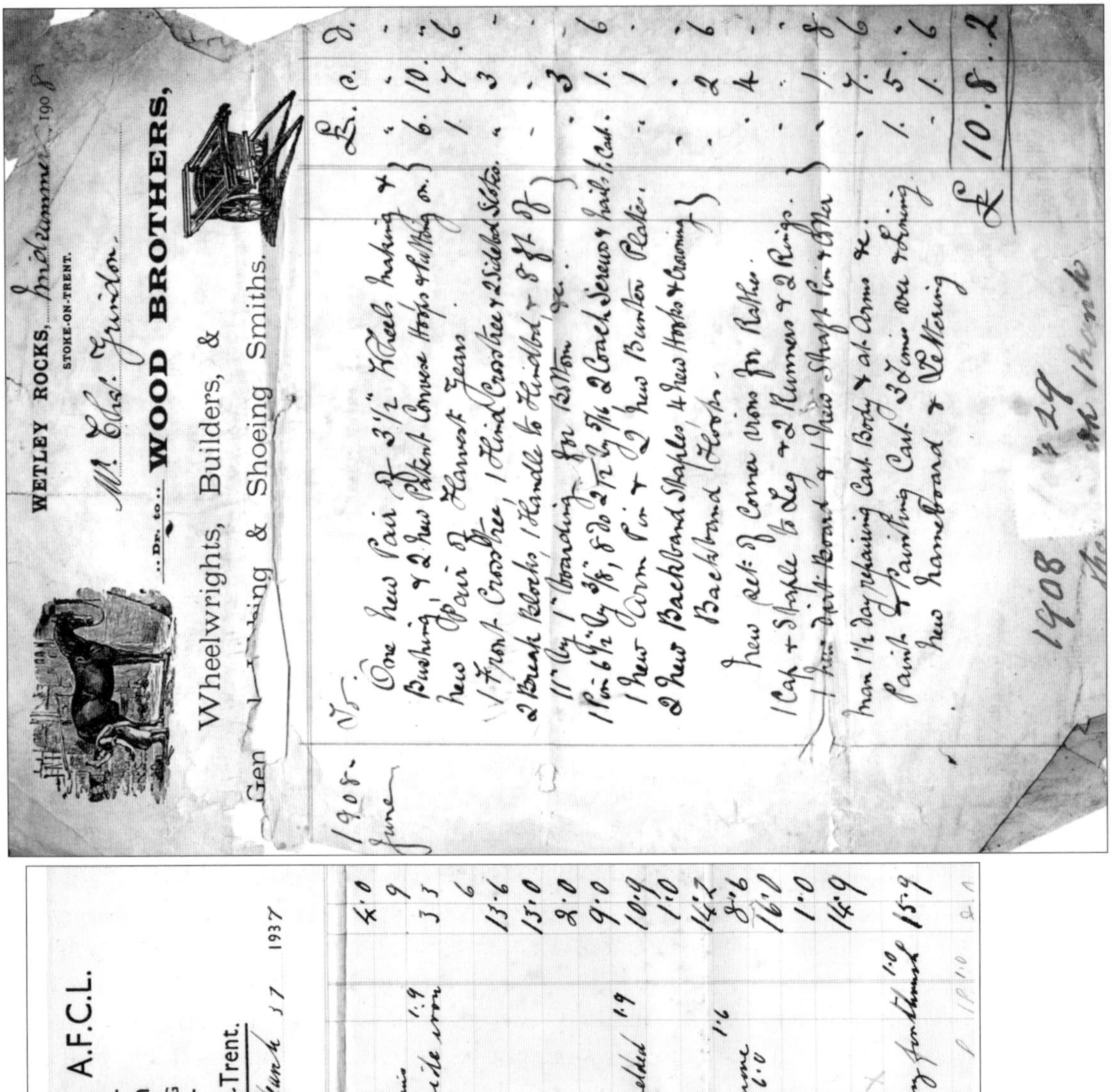

WETLEY ROCKS, Midsummer 1908
STOKE-ON-TRENT.

Mr. Chas. Grindon

..Dr. to.. WOOD BROTHERS,

Wheelwrights, Builders, &
General Smithing & Shoeing Smiths.

		£	s.	d.
1908 June	To			
	One new Pair of 3½" Wheels making & Bushing, & 2 new Patent Convese Hoops & Putting on.	6.	10.	-
	new Pair of Harvest Gears	1	7	6
	1 Front Crosstree, 1 Hind Crosstree & 2 Sidebd Slotes.	-	3	-
	2 Break Blocks, 1 Handle to Hindbd, & 8 ft of 11" by 1" boarding for Bottom &c.	-	3	-
	1 Pin 6½" by 3/8, 8 do 2½ by 5/16 2 Coach Screws & Nails, 1 Cast.	-	1.	6
	1 new Arm Pin & 2 new Bunter Plates.	-	1	-
	2 new Backband Staples, 4 new Hooks & Crowning Backband Hooks.	-	2	6
	new set of Corner irons for Rathes.	-	4	-
	1 Cap & Staple to Leg & 2 Runners & 2 Rings. 1 new dirt Board & 1 new Shaft Pin & Cotter	-	1.	8
	man 1½ day repairing Cart Body & at Arms &c.	-	7.	6
	Paint & Painting Cart 3 Times over & Lining	1.	5.	-
	new Nameboard & Lettering	-	1.	6
		£ 10.	8.	2

1908 [illegible] 29 ... thank

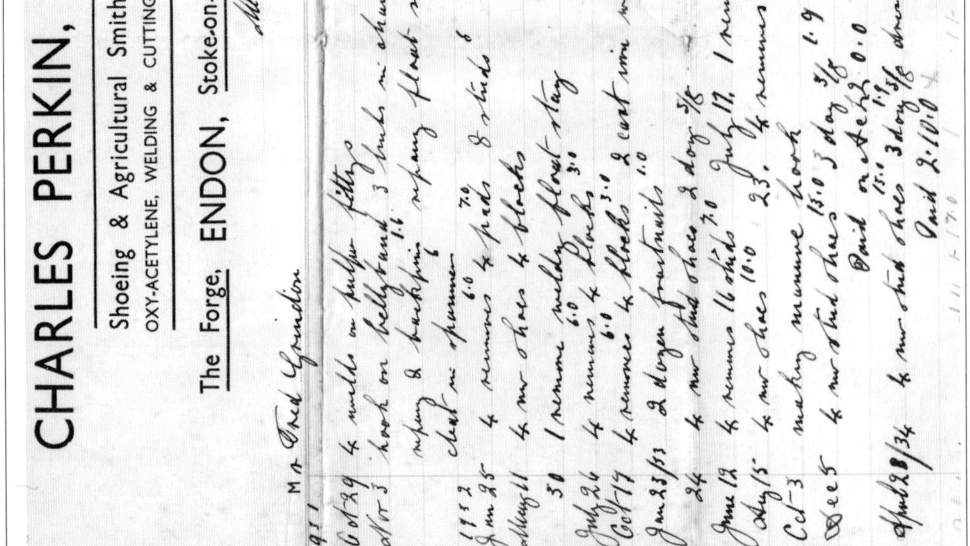

CHARLES PERKIN, A.F.C.L.

Shoeing & Agricultural Smith
OXY-ACETYLENE, WELDING & CUTTING

The Forge, ENDON, Stoke-on-Trent.

March 17 1937

Mr Fred Grindon

1951		
Oct 29	4 welds on pulper fittings	4.0
Nov 3	hook on bellyband 3 links in chains	9
	repairing & backpins 1.6 repairing float side iron 1.9	3 3
	cleat in spanner	6
1952 Jan 25	4 removes 6.0 4 pads 7.0 8 studs 6	13.6
May 11	4 new shoes 4 blocks	13.0
30	1 remove welding float stay	2.0
July 26	4 removes 6.0 4 blocks 3.0	9.0
Oct 17	4 removes 6.0 4 blocks 3.0 2 cart iron welded 1.9	10.9
Jan 23/53	2 dozen frostnails 1.0	1.0
24	4 new stud shoes 2 doz 3/8	14.2
June 12	4 removes 16 studs 7.0 July 17. 1 remove 1.6	8.6
Aug 15	4 new shoes 10.0 23. 4 removes 6.0	16.0
Oct 3	making manure hook	1.0
Dec 5	4 new stud shoes 13.0 3 doz 3/8 1.9	14.9
	Paid on Acct 2 0.0	
April 28/34	4 new stud shoes 15.0 3 doz 3/8 1.9 dressing for thrush 1.0	15.9
	Paid 2.10.0	

less packed up, lorries had taken over. The boatees liked a drink; on the way to Froghall, they'd stop at the Black Lion at Consall or the Boat at Cheddleton and then there was the Hollybush at Denford, but then it was very hard work.

The brickworks at Wallgrange were going strong when we were young, there were 30 to 40 blokes working there. Jack Spencer who lived on a little farm above the brickworks used to run a small lorry taking coal there; he just ran to the top side, tipped it down the bank and it ran down to the boiler house. Eventually I worked there for a couple of weeks getting bricks out of the kilns; it was a boiling hot job.

My brother-in-law, Reg Ferns worked in the marl hole for a good many years in all weathers. There were 3 or 4 of them and they had little wagons on a chain going down which they loaded up and it was taken up into the works, tipped over and then back again. It was all dug out by hand, mauling work especially in hot weather. Eventually the marl became too wet; it was normal to mix lime with it to dry it up, then it took too much lime and the bricks weren't good enough. I think that's why it finished.

When I was eight, I went to live with Mr and Mrs Corden up at Bluebell Farm, Park Lane. They hadn't got any children and they wanted some help. It was a lot further to walk to Longsdon School. I had to milk four cows, pump the water with a semi-rotary pump, 'mekson' out - if it was light enough, barrow the muck straight down the field and tip it in rucks. If it was dark it was tipped in a ruck in the farmyard.

Mr Corden worked on the railway at Wall Grange; he was a lengthsman on the line, his brother, Jim lived in the Station House, he was foreman and his wife was Station Master. I had to make sure the tyres were pumped up on his bike every morning before he went to work

It would take forty minutes or more to walk to school; it was hard work at first, and walking past home as well. Mr Corden's father lived up Denford near the top canal and I had to drop his milk off on the way in a billy can and pick the can up on the way back. Then do the same jobs again when I got back. They were long days but you never thought anything, just got on with it.

Mrs Corden's folks lived at Rownall Farm and I had to go across there on my bike in the holidays to do a bit of milking. On a Saturday, I had to go down to Coalpitford Farm, where Jack Reeves lived then, to pick a joint of meat up, because he worked at the butchers. Then clean all the hencotes out and scrub the yard. If it got very dry in summer and the well ran dry, we had to cart water from across Rose Bank with horse and cart. There was also a big garden to tend. In the old days it had been a pub.

I was there for 4 years till I was nearly 12, when I started secondary school at Endon; I went back home then. I left school at 15; I just missed out, they'd just put the leaving age up from 14.

Jake Hall was the road lengthsman; he lived round the 'corkscrew'. He swept the loose stone up, cleaned the grids out and kept the roadsides tidy with his wooden barrow, shovel and brush.

John Wain used to keep a cow and milk it out in the field. He used to tie it by the hedge and us lads used get the other side and tickle it with a stick to see if it would kick him. One Christmas morning, we got up and from the living room window we could see a body floating in the canal. When the police came we found out it was John Wain. We never knew what had happened, whether he'd fallen in after being in the Hollybush or if he'd thrown himself in.

Jim Davenport used to milk a cow and put the milk in a can which he took on a butcher's bike along the towpath and up to his brothers to go on the milk wagon. There could be 4 little pickups at one place.

Cousin Bill and Uncle Bill Grindon.

The New Inn, Longsdon.

Major Fitt lived at Micklea Farm and had a Guernsey cow and either me or dad had to go up and milk this cow every morning and night for quite a few years, unless the cow was dry of course. They reared a calf and made butter. I don't know if dad was paid but I didn't get anything.

Nearby was what I always took to be the parish quarry; I remember when Major Robinson built the bungalow on Denford Road, Frank Beech built the roadside wall and he went in the quarry and made the coping stones. When I was a lad, Major Robinson lived in the bungalow along Sandy Lane and I walked up and carried their drinking water from the well at the Intakes into a big bowl, two or three times a week. I got half a crown a time for that.

There were quite a few trains going through; if we were walking up the road and one was coming, we'd run onto the bridge and get covered in smoke and occasionally put a ha'penny on the track so it was squashed and made into a penny - or so we thought.

When I was working on the farm, we fetched beet pulp from Wall Grange station with tractor and trailer and put it in a clamp and trod it down for the winter. We had quite a few acres up on Mick Low where we grew 2 or 3 acres of corn, an acre of potatoes, turnips, kale and carrots. We used to get the potatoes by hand; me, dad and my brother. We'd pull the tops of a patch in the morning, dig them and let them dry, then put them in a heap and cover them with soil. Eventually we'd load them up, take them home and sort them, then sell them round the village in hundredweight bags. We'd have a day delivering; some would have one or two bags and we'd sell a few loose at home.

We sometimes had sewerage sludge from Leekbrook. Alf Wilshaw, who lived at Hazlehurst Cottage used to fetch it on his 30 cwt wagon. His brother was fetching it one day for Charlie Davenport and they'd got a track up through the wood to their top fields, but they couldn't get up; so he must have us with the tractor to pull him up. They got halfway, my brother was driving the tractor and the breasting wall collapsed and let them down. The lorry rolled over down the bank and they finished up with the back wheel of the tractor on the lorry cab. Luckily no-one was hurt much; Norman Wilshaw said it was like being in a washing machine tippling down the bank.

Dad used to have quite a bit of the sludge; it was weathered and not too unpleasant. They had to throw it off the wagon into a ruck, then we chucked it onto another trailor and put it out in smaller rucks, all by hand. It could grow tomato plants!

There was night-soil collection; a little wagon with a container on used to come round. I remember him coming to the Hollybush cottages. Sometimes they'd tip that out on dad's land, just run round and let it run out.

Albert Buckley and his wife used live at Canal Cottage and he used to mow the canal sides and we used to help him cart it back on a boat, throw it off and carry it up the batter and into the yard and make a stack of it. There was enough to keep a couple of cows. When Jim Davenport was there, he'd have a pig or two. He'd sold one to Fred Roberts as kept the New Inn pub. He wanted to feed it on swillings and stuff to get it bigger though it was quite a big pig already; six or seven score. He'd got a three wheeled truck with a wooden body on, so we put a pig net over the top and got this pig in. We had two or three goes, it kept rushing in and bursting the net and getting out. We managed to get it in eventually and set off across the canal towpath. Then going through one of the little gates, one wheel ran up the side and we tipped it over but eventually we got it right again and set off all the way across the canal, then pulled it all the way up Denford to the New Inn, me and my brother.

Fred Grindon, Denford in the late 1960s.

Probably Fred Grindon mowing the New Inn field in the 1930s.

The Hollybush and Hollybush cottages, Denford c.1970.

Jess Reeves about 1960.

John Reeves

My parents, Jack and Jess Reeves kept the Hollybush at Denford. When I was about ten in the mid 1950s I can remember that serving finished at ten o'clock on a Sunday night, so then they had a sing song for half an hour. There'd be a dozen or so and Harry Grindon usually set it off. I remember 'The Old Rugged Cross' and 'Bless this House' - and I was trying to get to sleep in the bedroom above.

Jack and John.

In the field opposite Grindon's, they held a couple of cricket matches. Frank Hewitt brought a side from Leek and the local lads challenged them. It was quite one-sided; we got beaten!

A local character was Fred Firkins; he used to have a spittoon under his seat when he sat in the corner of the smoke room near the fire and he used to spit in it about forty times during a Sunday dinner time. As he went to leave, if they gave him an extra pint, he'd sing a verse or two of 'The Old Rugged Cross'.

My grandad Bill Steers lived with us; I don't think he ever went out of Longsdon or Cheddleton in his life. He worked at Wall Grange brickworks as stoker on the kiln. He reckoned he fired the bricks for Leek Police Station on Leonard Street. He could drink a lot and one of his favourite games was Nine Card Don which he played most nights.

The beer was kept in about six barrels in the cellar and drawn by tap into gallon enamel jugs and carried up into the bar. In Wakes Week, when it was really busy, it was a full time job during opening hours for my uncle Bill Steers. He'd drop the filled jugs on the top step and dad would pick them up,

pour them out and put them back again. There'd be three or four continuously being filled.

I have some old plans dated 1907 which include a proposed tea room upstairs, a visitor's dining room, a row of cow stables and horse stables at the Hollybush. Next to the pub is shown Old Flour Mill, where the cottages are now.

One warm night three or four men came from inside to sit out. They must have startled the cat up the pear tree which grew up the front of

Fishermen at the Hollybush.

the pub. This caused it to piddle which must have hit every branch on the way down and showered the men below. They had to go to the canal and try and bathe it off.

There used to be bad floods in Denford, often twice a year until the water authorities made some flood defences. One August Bank Holiday, it was said that someone had left the lock gates at Hazelhurst open and the canal overflowed on the wrong side of the flood defences. When my brother Bill went home the water was up to the window sills and the dog was floating round on the settee.

John Reeves, Norman Green, Bill Reeves 1950.

LEFT: Jess and Jack Reeves with their grandchildren.

BELOW: The floods in the 1950s.

Dorothy Biddulph

I was born at Two Lands, School Lane Longsdon. My dad Bill Biddulph drove a steam roller for Staffs County Council apart from in winter, when he could be shovelling snow onto the back of a lorry if some needed clearing. My mum, Doris was the caretaker of Longsdon Primary School and she also worked in the canteen with Mrs Beech.

She kept four cows and milked them and had a little milk round locally; just a few houses. At first she took it in cans, then she had some milk bottles which had to be sterilised. She also sent a few gallons in a churn as well which was taken down to the corner of Devil's Lane on a homemade, four wheel truck. My brother Harry and I took it sometimes.

I started going to chapel when I was four; father sent Harry and I. Harry left when he was fourteen, but I stayed on because I really enjoyed it. I went to the Sunday School and became a member of the chapel when I was 18. It was well attended, we had a big stage to stand on for the anniversary services and there were concerts which Granny Heath put

Dad, Bill Biddulph.

together; they were really good. It was so popular it had to be done on two nights. There were jumble sales and coffee mornings as well. I remember Fred Mason was a very good Circuit Minister and John Sales was a local preacher who would bang the Bible down and dust would go every where, you'd nearly jump out of your skin.

There were Sunday School trips; we went on a coach to Pickmere Lake, Trentham Gardens, Alton Towers, which was different then - a bit of a fair and the gardens - and Drayton Manor Park. There was a bus full, parents went as well.

It was a good Sunday school, I became a teacher and I used to enjoy working along with the children doing craft work. I liked the special services like Easter, Harvest, Christmas and the Anniversary; I enjoyed the hymns.

Dorothy Knight started a Girl Guide group; they kept asking me to join but I didn't think I should, I'd just left school then. Anyway I did join and eventually Dorothy went abroad and it left me helping out and learning at the same time which wasn't very easy. We met at Longsdon Church room and at the chapel room every Tuesday evening except in school

Mum, Doris Corbishley at a dairy competition, Leek Butter Market, 1920s.

Dad's steamroller
at Two Lands.

Dad's last job - taken at the bottom of Ash Bank.

In Longsdon chapel.

Chapel Sunday School about 1967, and below about 1965.

Left: Missionary Queen, 1949, Leek Methodist Circuit.

Right: Harry, Mum and me 1945.

holidays. We started with 14 girls and got up to 20 odd; we did knots and badges which included laundry and home-maker.

When they went off on camps, I didn't go because you had to have a certificate. Some of them went with other companies. We once had one night when we camped in a field at Great Longsdon but that night I had no sleep, they were too noisy, then when it was time to get up and get breakfast they were all asleep. I had started making the camp fire and cooking over it - they were ready to eat when I woke them up.

I was Acting Lieutenant, then Lieutenant, Acting Captain then Captain; I finished after 30 odd years. Sometimes I didn't enjoy it; there only had to be one girl to lead the others astray and I couldn't control them, then I worried, but when they were a good crowd, it was great.

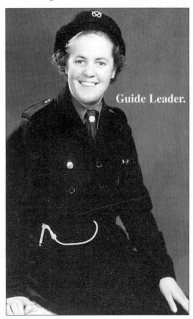

Guide Leader.

We once went in for the National Song contest but got knocked out at Stafford. The Brownies got through and ended up coming second nationally. It was a wonderful experience. I went to London with them; we had to sleep in a big room in sleeping bags. One little brownie didn't like being on her own and snuggled down with me in my sleeping bag. I didn't get much sleep that night. When we got back to Longsdon, they put a Welcome Home banner up and a buffet on for us.

There were Cubs and Scouts as well and we all had a parade together once a month, one month at St Chads and the other at chapel with flags and everything, the chapel was filled.

Another village event was 'Welcome Yule'. Mrs Hall from Ladderedge had a lot to do with organising it. We all came on singing 'Here we come a wassailing among the leaves so green' dressed in black cloaks. Then when we got onto the stage we reversed them and we'd all got different colours. We sang carols. It was held at the Memorial Hall every year for some time. The Walker family were very musical and were often involved in things, Harold and his son Roger would play piano duets.

There were pantomimes as well, Betty Bunting helped with those - *Aladdin, Cinderella, Jack and the Beanstalk*. These ended and there was a big show called *March Madness*, mostly musical, a really good show. Sylvia Godwin's School of Dance took part. The village was alive, there was so much going on then.

Chapel Sunday School about 1970.

Longsdon School 1954.

Longsdon School 1921.

AD Stewart (head), Arthur Brown, Edward Bentley, Alfred Owen, Reg Embrey, George Dutton, Alan Edge, Cecil Ashley, Marge Robinson (teacher)
Madge Rhodes, Ethel Knight, Jessie Sant, Annie Byatt, Dolly Brindley, Lizzie Wooliscroft, Dolly Heath, Mary Cope.
Lily Tait, Vera Cope, Maggie McKnight, Grace Heath, George Brooks, Charlie Cope, Billy Hammersley, Tom Bentley.
Front; Lawrence Bailey, Frank Saunders, Stanley Hilditch, Tom Bray, Reg Bunting, Bill Smith, Rowland Embrey, Harold Heath.

Longsdon School 1920s.

Dorothy Biddulph, Eva Davenport, Eileen Beaumont, June Sant, Evelyn Briggs, Barbara Beech, Beryl Johnson, Sheila Mellor..

Above: Longsdon schoolchildren.
BACK: Gordon Yates, June Stubbs, Evelyn Briggs, Marjorie Brown, Marcia Stubbs, Mary Smith.
MIDDLE: Shirley Stubbs, Freda Beech, June Sant, Christine Beech, Pearl Gritton, Dorothy Biddulph.
FRONT: Ann Martin, Agnes Wise, Josephine Ratcliffe.

Longsdon Pet Show 1960s.
Brenda Heath, Louise Stubbs, Graham Hill, Peter Hill, Eileen Hill.

James Wood Myatt

I was born at Close Gate Farm, my Father was George Myatt and he bought the farm in 1927 just before he married my Mother, Alice Wood. My Mother liked to tell the story about when on the day of their wedding a long rope was tied across the Hall Bank not allowing them to get to Church; they had to pay a toll to let them pass. It was a custom wishing them good luck.

Alice Myatt.

George Myatt Senr.

My brother George was born four years after me. A lot of the family lived locally; my Mother's sister Elsie lived next door at Hallgate, my Uncle Charlie Myatt next to that at Gratton Hall. Mothers parents lived at Bradshaw Farm and my Father's parents retired from Gratton Hall to Holly Villa next to the Chapel.

I attended Horton School from the age of 5; it was where the Village Hall is now. Apart from reading and writing we had other chores such as carrying the water from the well, shovelling coal for the school boiler and tending the school garden. When the War came we had another chore; one of us would be on air raid duty standing outside to listen for the siren from Cheddleton or Leek. If it went off we all had to get down on the floor. The War also brought the evacuees from Manchester and London. We took in two brothers, Harry & Arthur Turner. Arthur didn't stay long, he went back with his parents after one of their visits. Harry stayed for a couple of years and wasn't much trouble except for when he slipped in the cow drinking pool on the way back from Chapel one Sunday.

There were two evacuees at my Aunts at Hallgate, Bill Kennedy and his sister, they also came from Manchester. Bill had a very good voice and went on to sing in choirs. He visited a few years ago and could remember travelling from Manchester to Rudyard by train where he was met by my Aunt with her horse and cart. He could remember a plane crashing at Dunwood and running across the fields to go and look at it. Whilst the evacuees were staying they attended Horton school - they went in the morning whilst we went in the afternoon as the school wasn't big enough for all of us.

My Mother Alice Wood was one of three sisters; the others were Elsie and Jessie. They also had a brother James (Jim) who lived at Rudyard and was the local Co-op Insurance man. Their parents were William and Harriet Minnie Wood. Harriet was the niece of George Heath the Moorland Poet; I can remember scrubbing his gravestone at Horton Church.

My Mother and Aunt Elsie would take the horse and cart to Leek to sell eggs; the horse lived for about 35 years before it had to be put down. Occasionally I stayed at Hallgate; I remember mice moving the pillow under my head.

After Horton School I went to Mountside School for boys in Leek. I left at the age of 14 and went to work on the farm. On my last day I got the cane for getting into a fight. I would help milk the cows by hand; we had about 20 shorthorns. In the winter I would help to feed and muck them out; we also had to fetch water for them from the brook as there was no piped water until the 1950s. Harold Nixon came to work on the farm and became part of the family as he carried on working for us for 46 years. He married Lily and they lived at Shortcroft which is now Toll Gate. Harold would walk over the fields to work or sometimes he

Harold Nixon, Bill and Jim Myatt.

would bike to work on his moped. Later Harold and Lily and their family moved to Ivy Dene in Gratton.

The milk was stored in churns and cooled in the yard waiting for Bob Heathcote to collect with his wagon and take them to Manchester. So many times a year a Jewish Rabbi came in a big black coat by car from Manchester to bless the milk. It would then be kept separate and labelled Kosher before going on the wagon.

My brother George married Hilda Hall and they moved to Woodcock Hurst Farm at Endon. I met Phyllis Wood from Rushton and we married in 1962; we had a son and three daughters and continued to live at Close Gate Farm. We had a good community and always had lots of help at haymaking time from our neighbours, the Hills, Nixons and Harrisons.

Stan Gordon

We lived at Dams Lane Farm, Gratton from where my father ran two cattle wagons and when I was 17, I started to drive one of them. We could take the sides off and make a flat lorry, so on a Monday I'd go to Newcastle Market, then take the cattle body off and on Tuesday go to Liverpool to fetch 8 tons of corn in bags for Williamsons at Endon. Then put the body back on for Leek market on Wednesday and again to Leek on Thursday for the 'graders', the fat stock and on Friday take the body off again and go to Liverpool for another load of corn.

There wasn't much room when the market was in the middle of Leek; the pens were always full. We had to take a load of stock in, then wash out before loading again. I took some cows in one Thursday morning for Ben Edge from Sprinks Farm at Horton. We unloaded them and one got away and ran up Derby Street. We were running after it and it went into a shop. A lad was on his bike and Ben ran into him and knocked him off it.

Some Fridays there were horse sales and on one occasion there was a horse which a farmer from Rushton had bought. He was known for getting drunk and had gone in the ring and bid for this horse so Mr Ash the auctioneer asked me to deliver it to his farm. When I got there and pulled the ramp down to unload this horse the farmer said *'I haven't bought it.'* I replied, *'Mr Ash says you have and I'd to deliver it here. 'No!'* he says, turning nasty; he was going to attack me. *'You can take it back!'* I said, *'If I'm going back, you're coming with me.'*

So we went back to Leek and he tried to jump out of the lorry on one corner. When we got there Mr Ash said to him, *'It was knocked down to you, you've got to pay for it.'* So they agreed and as soon as I knew the deal was done I went with the horse and just drew onto his farm and let the horse go and left the farmer in Leek to make his own way home in return for him being nasty to me.

Sometimes from the market a cow would need to be slaughtered straight away, or we could have a mad bull on the lorry and we had to deliver them to the old slaughter house in Pump Street. It was all very narrow and we had to back all the way down the street and right up so you could drop the ramp and they could get a rope round their head and pull them straight in.

The butchers in Leek had a field on Abbey Green Road near to the houses by the bridge. They could drop sheep or cattle off there from market then when they wanted to kill one we had to pick it up there and take it to the abattoir. I think the butchers owned it between them.

We had a partition in the front of the wagon and took calves into Newcastle or Leek. We only charged half a crown to pick them up and the farmers would put a piece of string round their necks with a churn label on with their name and address so you knew whose calves they were. But by the time you got to market the calves had sucked the labels off and you didn't know which belonged to who; you had to guess. Sometimes the farmers wanted a lift in to the market and you could have more farmers in the front than cows in the back.

We moved up to Cheddleton and started a haulage business getting up to 6 lorries but not in the farm trade. When dad retired and sold the lorries, I kept three and moved to Rudyard and my wife kept the shop and Post Office there.

I had once delivered a load of bagged lime to Liverpool and rang to the Clearing House to get a load back. They'd got a boat load of timber at the docks which had to be got to Wragby in Lincolnshire to a sawmill. So I loaded these two pieces of timber weighing between 15 and 16 tons and brought them home and parked on the Station Hotel car park ready to deliver the next day. A Leek Post photographer saw me there and took this picture. It was a big load in those days, the mid sixties.

Jessie Gordon with one of the first Land Rovers.

Stan Gordon age 18 at
Gratton.

Thornycroft lorry 1953-54.

BELOW:
Stan Gordon at the Station
Hotel, Rudyard.

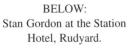

Peter Dzik

It's many years since I first found St Michael's Church in Horton, on a day out touring the hills around Rushton and Horton. I enjoyed the idyllic rural views, the well kept graveyard and the serenity of the church's interior. There is an interesting grave of Mary Brooks who died in 1787 at 119 years of age. Only much later doing family history research did I find Yardley ancestors buried there. And because I enjoy history I read quite a bit about Leek and the Moorlands, including the *History of Horton Hall*. One item I had found was about a Quaker called William Yardley of Dairyhouse, Horton, who had been imprisoned in Leek jail in 1655 during the English republic of Oliver Cromwell. So began a search down the centuries and across the Atlantic. He seems unknown in North Staffordshire history, yet he is important in Pennsylvania and Quaker history.

William was a key leader in the preparation and first settlements in Pennsylvania of the persecuted Quakers of England. 28 ships were involved in the miserable 60 day crossing of the Atlantic in 1682, made up partly of Leek and Moorlands folk and nearby south Cheshire colleagues. Yardley had married Jane Heath, one of three Heath sisters from Horton who married Quaker preachers and emigrated to America. It's not clear whether these sisters are from Heathhouse farm or Blackwood, but there were four Heath families in Horton at the time, with more in Endon. There are many ancestors of the other two sisters, but the three Yardley/Heath Horton born adult sons died in an epidemic in late 1702 in Pennsylvania.

Two of William Yardley's younger nephews, Thomas and Richard, were sent over in 1704 to sort out the lands, and stayed to have many children. The town of Yardley, Bucks County, Pennsylvania is named after them. Back in Horton, William's four brothers and sisters had many descendants who spread across the Moorlands - Eardleys, Malkins, Wilshaws ,Unwins .etc

Going back in time I found out about the Yardley coat of Arms plus one of their Cheshire cousins who had been on major pirate expeditions to the Spanish West Indies in Queen Elizabeth's time. And we shouldn't forget outlaw Roger Heath of Horton c1480, concerning a murder of the Edge family of Horton Hall. There might even be a Horton link to John Heath who was lynched in, of all places, Tombstone, Arizona in 1884. He had been involved in rustling and robbery and been a deputy sheriff but then went back to outlaw ways. His 5 man gang was hung the following day.

There is also a royal connection for those distant relatives who wish to claim a free week's B & B at Windsor Castle. Alice Yardley's Charity of Rushton Spencer still exists after 350 years she died c.1653, aged about 76. Her parents were Edward Sutton of Rushton Hall and Anne Stanley of the widespread Stanley family of Lancashire, one of the most powerful medieval English families but who had originated from Stanley, only 5 miles away from Horton. The family included the Earl of Derby who got the title by his army deciding the Battle of Bosworth in 1485, which brought the Tudors to the throne. There must have been Staffordshire Moorlands men involved in the Battle because the actual killer of King Richard III was Ralph Rudyard of Rudyard, one of the knights of Lord Stanley. Part of the Stanley ancestry goes back to William, brother of King Richard Lionheart and King John.

And just to let you know how awkward life was in older times, some Yardleys were master hatmakers in Newcastle under Lyme. The curing of felt for the hats required soaking it in heated mercury. This rots the brain, hence the term 'mad as a hatter'. However, one popular side effect was sexual stimulation similar to Viagra. Hence King Charles II had his own laboratory, partly to assist his orgies. He was found dead in it, allegedly dying from an excess while snorting-in his last mercury heating.

Bond House Farm, Horton.

Maurice and Reg Heath at Bond House.

Horton and Rudyard ladies.

Arthur Corbishley, Horton 1982. The last person in the area to farm with a Standard Fordson and a Bamlett trailer mower.

Horton school late 1950s, Lichfield Cathedral Appeal.

BELOW: Horton 1950s.

Ancient Order of Foresters.

Horton Hall.

Mr Stubbs and Mr Birkinshaw.

The first committee at Horton Village Hall, at a concert.

Horton Old School

Horton Choir
Marion Hill, Nancy Heath, Margaret Heath, -- --,
Nellie Pitcher, -- Gaskill, Elsie Goodhall.

Horton New School

Father Eric Tomlinson - Vicar of Horton, Longsdon, Rushton Spencer

My first experience of actually living in the countryside was becoming Vicar of Horton, Longsdon and Rushton Spencer 16 years ago. That's not to say I'd never been in villages you understand, or didn't know what grass was. Indeed, in my early twenties, at the one and only time of my being a Best Man at a wedding in Herefordshire, I actually milked a cow by hand would you believe!

Nevertheless, I have to say that leaving the industrial sprawl of the Black Country and the urban mass of Wolverhampton where I had been Vicar for the previous fifteen years, and entering the peace and quiet tranquility of the countryside was both delightful - and also a bit of a shock. Why? Well, despite the fact that the location of the house of my earliest childhood is buried somewhere beneath the giant concrete supports that hold up Junction 9 of the M6, I have never actually lived so close to such a busy road as the A53 - the Longsdon autobahn that runs through the 'village'.

In towns the streets are always very well lit and all the houses are more or less joined-up. More wonderfully still, they all have numbers! The odds on the left and the evens on the right. In our three villages, but especially Horton and Rushton Spencer, there is the pretty, but frustrating arrangement whereby the houses are not so much joined up but scattered all over the place; some of them are half a mile from everybody else - on their own, yes, even occupying their own 'street'! They might be easier to find if all the names were at least re-arranged into alphabetical order.

During my first six months here I was regularly amazingly puzzled in the pursuit of finding Gratton. Now there are signs on several lanes indicating Gratton 2 miles. But there was never a sign to tell you that you were actually in Gratton. During those very early months I learned that Gratton had a more effective and illuminated signpost than anything the SMDC could have erected. It was the delightful Barbara Hill and her little bonfires on the crossroads. Wonderful! Often I'd stop and have a natter with her and Reg. Then I'd pause and think. Imagine stopping in the middle of the crossroads in Wolverhampton. Better still, imagine lighting a fire there!

Rush hour traffic is an ever-present feature of urban dwelling. I suppose the nearest we get to such a thing in the countryside is meeting a herd of cows on a lane. It reminds me of an occasion during my very first month here. It was a lovely sunny morning and I had turned left at the bottom of Dunwood Lane to go up to Horton Church when my gaze was frozen on a two-ton lump of bull strolling along the lane towards me. (Not a familiar sight in Wolverhampton!) Everywhere seemed isolated; not another soul around. Just the bull and me - the space between us reducing at his every ponderous step. In strangled panic I mobile telephoned farmer Eric Gilman whose re-assuring advice was: *'well, you dunna want worry. 'E anna 'urtin anybody is 'e!'*

During my first weeks here I recall leaning on a wall admiring the Highland cattle near Frank Sutton's Garage at Rudyard. A local Horton man came by and I commented to him how absolutely beautiful it is round here. His reply was very deep; *'Ah it is. An' dunna yo get tellin' anybody abaht it either!'* I've never forgotten those wise words. For unlike the Lake District or Cotswolds with their coach-loads of tourists, it is the quiet unspoilt naturalness of the Moorlands which is the secret of its unique beauty. And it might indeed be because *'we dunna tell anybody abaht it'*.

Truly, the Moorlands countryside is beautiful - even its smells and muddy lanes. And yet, uncontaminated by the neon haze of city streets, its greatest majesty is when it is shrouded by the dark pall of soft night. In the silence we are called to look up and glorify:

'How the floor of heaven is thick inlaid with patens of bright gold. There's not the smallest orb which thou behold'st but in his motion like an angel sings still quiring to the young-ey'd cherubins.' (Romeo & Juliet) .... and thus in awesome prayer conclude, *'Deo gratias!'*

Yew Tree House, originally bought for the Curate, became the Longsdon Vicarage.

In 1899 John Robinson of Westwood Hall gave land for a burial ground and in 1901 adjoining land for the new church, completed in 1905. The curate's house was enlarged and a parish room added to become the vicarage. The provision of church, burial ground, house and parish room was described as 'one of the most complete gifts that the diocese of Lichfield has ever known'. (*Victoria County History*)

LADDEREDGE.

Particulars of Sale and Plan

OF A VERY DESIRABLE

FREEHOLD RESIDENCE

AND

LAND,

KNOWN AS

YEW TREE HOUSE,

WHICH WILL BE SOLD BY AUCTION BY

MR. JOSHUA MILLWARD,

At the George Hotel, in Leek,

On Wednesday, 25th April, 1888,

AT 4 O'CLOCK PUNCTUALLY.

Mr. Myatt, the owner and occupier, will shew the property, and Particulars and any further information may be had on application to the Auctioneer, Longnor, Buxton, or

CHALLINOR & CO.,

SOLICITORS, LEEK.

Rev. Warren, the curate from All Saints, Leek was ordained the first vicar of Longsdon.

The Queen is Miss Warren.

At the Church Room.
Rev. Warren and his wife on right, their son to his left, and their daughter on right of front row.